W9-BEP-241

PUTTING YOUR EMPLOYEES
First

The ABCs for Leaders of
Generations X, Y, & Z

MICHAEL BERGDAHL

simple **truths**
▶ Our Goal is to Help You Reach Yours.

Copyright © 2018 by Michael Bergdahl

Cover and internal design © 2018 by Sourcebooks, Inc.

Cover design by Heather Morris/Sourcebooks, Inc.

Internal images © HerminUtomo/Getty Images, Misha Petrishchev/Noun Project, LAFS/Noun Project, Alice Noir/Noun Project, LINE ICONS/Shutterstock, Pensiri/Shutterstock

Published by Simple Truths, an imprint of Sourcebooks, Inc.

P.O. Box 4410, Naperville, Illinois 60567-4410

(630) 961-3900

Fax: (630) 961-2168

sourcebooks.com

Library of Congress Cataloging-in-Publication data is on file with the publisher.

Printed and bound in China.

QL 10 9 8 7 6 5 4 3 2 1

||||||||||||||||||||||||||||||

**The true worth of your leadership
legacy will be judged, measured,
and remembered based upon
how well you treated the people
around you along the way.**

||||||||||||||||||||||||||||||

*To my multigenerational family members, who
selflessly and patiently supported, guided, and
influenced me to become the person I am today:*

*William "Bill" Bergdahl Sr. & Ellen Strom Bergdahl,
my paternal grandparents
Edward "Biffy" Autio & Rachel Maki Autio,
my maternal grandparents
Robert "Bob" Bergdahl Sr. and Elaine "Gingy" Autio
Bergdahl, my parents
Sheryl DeYoung Bergdahl, my wife
Heather Lynn Bergdahl, my daughter
Paul Michael Bergdahl, my son*

CONTENTS

'LL NEVER FORGET THE employee relations and leadership experience I had in the days following the September 11, 2001 terrorist attacks in New York City. At that time, I worked for a *Fortune* 500 company with operations throughout the New York City metropolitan area.

As the concerned leadership team of an organization with many employees impacted, we asked the question, *What can we possibly do at a time like this to support our employees?* The only strategy we thought made any sense was to reach out to them, support them emotionally during that difficult time, and simply show compassion. With the advice of professional grief counselors, our company's leaders decided to proactively hold group and one-on-one meetings with all our NYC-area employees to get them to talk openly about what had happened.

Once we'd made that decision, I drove all night from my home to New York (370 miles) to conduct those meetings. The reason I had to drive was because all the airlines were shut down for several days following the attack. When I arrived at five a.m., I only had time to check into my hotel in Brooklyn before heading straight out to begin employee meetings at seven that morning.

In the aftermath of the attacks, I conducted multiple employee-support meetings in Brooklyn, the Bronx including Harlem River Yard, and across our company locations on Long Island. Many of our employees had personally witnessed the plane hitting the second World Trade Center tower from vantage points around NYC, and they had watched firsthand, in horror, as the Twin Towers came crashing down. Like the rest of the world, our employees were filled with the mixed emotions of anger, grief, and sadness as they mourned the deaths of so many innocent victims.

One of the employee assistance meetings that a trained grief counselor and I conducted stands out in my mind. We had an operation at a facility called BQE, named because of its physical proximity to the Brooklyn-Queens Expressway. In fact, our BQE facility was located directly under the elevated section of the roadway. On September 14, 2001, we conducted an employee assistance meeting in the shadows under the expressway with cars and trucks roaring across the highway overhead. I can still picture that surreal setting in my mind as if it were yesterday.

What made this employee meeting even more memorable was the work group to which we were presenting. This particular group of approximately one hundred employees was all Spanish speaking (the majority non-English speaking). Fortunately, we had a Spanish-speaking interpreter to help us communicate. Because we didn't have a meeting room at BQE, we held the meeting outside in the parking lot, with all of us standing under the noisy expressway.

My Tribute Is to the Resiliency of People Everywhere

The indomitable human spirit always endures, even when people are facing monumental adversity, soul-crushing emotional trauma, overwhelming life changes, and an unclear path forward.

Like so many others in the New York City area, our employees had been personally and directly affected by the 9/11 attacks. Employees told us that neighbors, friends, family members, and first responders they knew personally had perished in the attacks. As we made our presentation, I saw my employees, both men and women, crying uncontrollably. Many of them came forward immediately following the meeting to talk directly with the grief counselor; many others expressed appreciation to us for taking the time to show concern by speaking with them.

Every company's executives, managers, and supervisors can learn valuable lessons from this story that could transform their company culture, the way they lead their team, and their relationship with each of their employees. The question is, *When was the last time you focused all your time, energy, and attention on your company's most important asset—your people?* In the twenty-first century, many of the most successful companies and leaders focus on the development, success, and happiness of their employees as their first priority.

That's because they know focusing on employees is not only good for business and good for customers, but it is also the right thing to do. They know engaged employees will enthusiastically take ownership of manufacturing, selling, and distributing products, while at the same time making customer service their highest priority. Not surprisingly, effective leaders know that strong sales and profitability will follow, and when employee morale is high, employee retention also improves.

It shouldn't take some kind of catastrophic event to cause a company's leaders to begin showing concern for their own employees. Effective leaders already exhibit that kind of caring, concerned, and compassionate leadership behavior each and every day.

That's what this book *Putting Your Employees First* is all about!

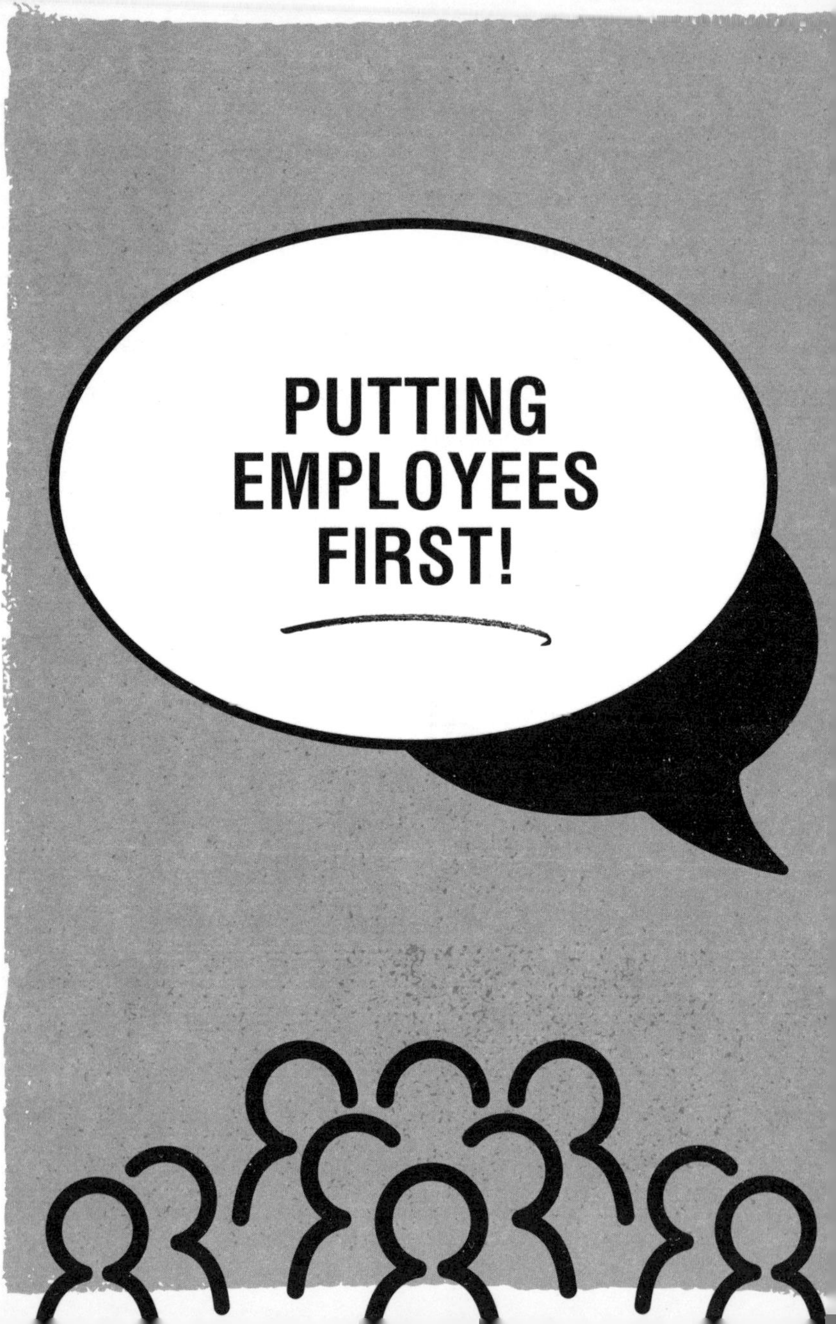
PUTTING EMPLOYEES FIRST!

If you treat your staff well, they will be happy. Happy staff are proud staff, and proud staff deliver excellent customer service, which drives business success.

—RICHARD BRANSON, VIRGIN GROUP

‖‖‖‖‖‖‖‖‖‖‖‖‖‖‖‖‖‖‖‖‖‖

Which kind of leader are you? Are you a leader employees love, respect, and enjoy being around, or are you the kind of leader they despise, disrespect, and can't wait to get away from at the end of the day?

‖‖‖‖‖‖‖‖‖‖‖‖‖‖‖‖‖‖‖‖‖‖

IT'S NOT HARD TO guess which one you'd prefer to be. Almost everyone who assumes a leadership position wants to be respected and even liked by the employees who report to them. *So why is it that so many leaders fail to bridge the relationship gap with their own team members?*

Part of the answer to that question lies in the fact that times have changed. In the past, employees put up with old-school authoritative, autocratic, and even dictatorial styles of leadership. They endured those unacceptable styles of leadership out of fear they might lose their job. This is a new day, and the current generations of employees look at the working world differently. Those old-school bullying styles of leadership simply don't work today, and in retrospect, they were never very effective.

The days of working cradle to grave for a single employer are long gone. Employees in the twenty-first century will quit their job the first chance they get to go to another company that they believe will treat them better and look out for their career interests. Even employees who like their jobs will quit if they don't feel that their current supervisor appreciates their work!

Employees today are demanding positive leadership from a leader and a company that recognize the value of employees. It's tough enough to recruit and hire good people; your company can't afford to lose them because of poor leadership. In the past, rather than fix the problem, employers would simply go out at a great expense and hire a new employee. That shortsighted strategy simply won't work today.

With social networking and internet sites dedicated to displaying reviews of what it's like to work for your company (see glassdoor.com) and even individual supervisors (for examples, see iratemyboss.com or ebosswatch.com), word gets around fast. Unfortunately, if the perception of you or your company isn't so positive, you'll find it tough to hire quality staff. On the other hand, if you and your company are perceived positively, prospective new employees will seek you out as an *employer of choice*. An important question to ask yourself is this: *How would your current employees rate your company and you as a leader?*

Employee Online Reviews of Their Supervisor

Prospective employees can read reviews of a company and its supervisors written by current employees. These evaluations can determine whether potential job applicants will actually apply for open positions.

Here are sample supervisor evaluation statements:

1. I feel like there is open and honest communication between my boss and me.
2. I feel like my boss cares about me as a person.
3. I feel like my boss cares about my career development.
4. I trust and respect my boss.
5. I like working for my boss.
6. I recommend this person as a good boss to work for.

With that background in mind, the recurring themes of this book are *effective leadership, putting employees first, employee engagement,* and *employee-centered culture.* As you read, I want to challenge you to consider adopting a *Putting Employees First leadership philosophy.*

To help you accomplish that goal, most of this book is

written around the Actions, Beliefs, and Competencies (referred to from now on as the ABCs) of leaders, with special emphasis on engagement of today's highly diverse and multi-generational employees. I will also discuss the merits of an *employee-centered culture*, which is a people strategy that focuses all individuals, programs, processes, and systems on helping employees become even more successful.

Based on my own experience as a human resources executive working for great leaders who acted as my mentors, I will share my knowledge and experience with you. I've worked in a variety of industries including: a summer job with a local municipal government, a restaurant while in college, a family-owned publishing company, a privately owned petrochemical company, an industry-leading consumer packaged-goods company, a shopping mall–based publicly traded specialty retailer, the world's largest discount retailer, and a solid waste disposal and recycling company.

Specifically, I will share what I learned regarding the challenges and benefits of engaging diverse and multi-generational employees regardless of the industry. In addition, the lessons I will provide are the same for effective leadership of employees whether their jobs are in sales, customer service, manufacturing distribution, or office staff, and whether they work at headquarters or in a field location, plant, or warehouse.

You'll find as you read that the primary focus of this book is YOU. Whether you are an entrepreneur, CEO, president, manager, or frontline supervisor, I want you to come away with a burning desire to become a better and more effective leader. Once you've finished reading, you may even decide to refocus your company's culture by adopting an *employee-centered cultural philosophy.*

I will discuss three leadership core values and ten key leadership competencies that are designed to address what diverse and multigenerational employees want and expect from their company's leadership. The three values are focused on respect, trust, and support. The ten key leadership competencies are: empowerment, mentoring, listening, approachability, empathy, integrity, acknowledgment, communication, high expectations, and leading by example. I'll discuss the three values and the ten key leadership competencies at length in later chapters.

As you read this book, I want you to mentally assess your own style of leadership. I'll provide opportunities for you to reflect upon your personal leadership actions, beliefs, and competencies, in addition to providing a self assessment you can take online to review how committed you truly are to putting your employees first.

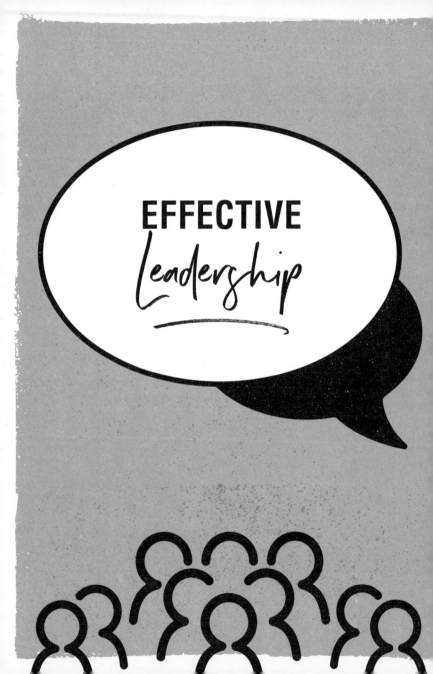

||||||||||||||||||||||||||||

The best leaders share several common traits, including commitment, integrity, a good attitude, a strong work ethic, and a sincere concern for people.

||||||||||||||||||||||||||||

Let's take a moment to look at *leadership expectations* from an employee perspective. When employees are asked to describe the attributes of *their best supervisor*, their lists often include descriptors like:

Looks out for me	*Knows who I am*	*Believes in me*
Listens to me	*Rewards me*	*Has high standards*
Is likeable	*Respects me*	*Recognizes me*
Gives feedback	*Supports the team*	*Is reliable*
Delegates work	*Easy to talk to*	*Has a positive outlook*
Cares about me	*Open and honest*	

The common threads running through this list are interpersonal and motivational "soft" skills like empathy, respect, listening, honesty, friendliness, caring, inspiring, and motivating. The best supervisors prove through their ABCs that the people around them are important and that, as leaders, they are worthy of being followed. Interestingly, this *best supervisor list* captures many of the same traits and attributes often used to describe effective business leaders.

Somewhat surprisingly, what employees want hasn't changed in almost seventy years, according to a survey conducted by Lawrence Lindahl in 1949.[1] In Lindahl's original research, employees were asked to force rank *what is most important to them*. Separately, managers were asked to force rank the same list based on *what they thought was most important to employees*. Below are those two lists comparing employee versus manager perceptions of *what is most important to employees*.

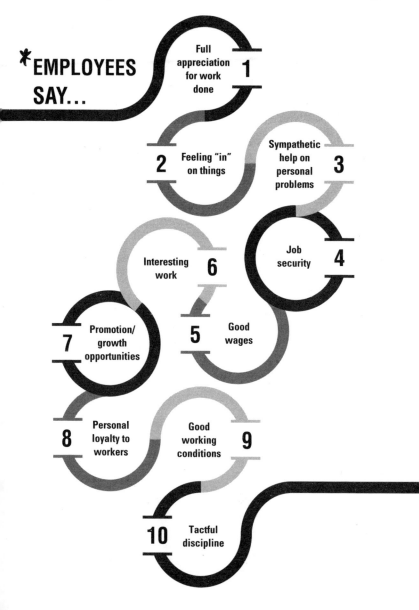

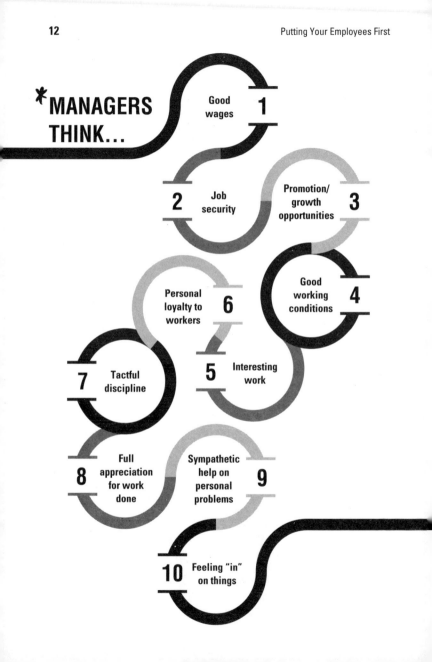

*MANAGERS THINK...

1 Good wages

2 Job security

3 Promotion/growth opportunities

4 Good working conditions

6 Personal loyalty to workers

5 Interesting work

7 Tactful discipline

8 Full appreciation for work done

9 Sympathetic help on personal problems

10 Feeling "in" on things

By comparing the two lists, you can clearly see there is a discrepancy between how employees and managers rank their perceptions. The top three on the employee list indicate the importance of managers having people skills like empathy, communications, caring, concern, and understanding. By comparison, the top three on the manager list are focused on wages, job security, and promotional opportunities. These differences in perception are particularly important for managers and supervisors to understand in order to bridge the employee engagement gap. As a leader, if you can tune in to what your employees really want and meet their needs, your chances of attracting, retaining, and motivating people will be greatly improved.

Employee expectations are actually quite reasonable: they want to do meaningful work, to receive recognition for a job well done, and to be kept informed.

During my twenty-five-year human resources career, I gained valuable experience in a variety of industries. My HR résumé includes stints at four *Fortune* 1000 companies, a billion-dollar privately held manufacturing firm, and a small family-owned company. Interestingly, only one of the companies where I worked openly embraced and promoted putting employees first. That company had an *employee-centered culture*. All the leaders there were held to a strict standard of looking out for and supporting the needs of employees. As an HR executive, that standard made my job a little bit easier, because everyone shared my HR passion for treating people right. By putting employees first, the company's leaders shifted the attention away from their own selfish, bottom-line interests and instead focused selflessly on the needs of employees.

That *employee-centered culture* was fully supported, promoted, and driven by the top executives. The CEO, a great people leader, was the company's greatest cheerleader for promoting the idea of taking care of and supporting the needs of employees. The CEO embraced a set of values and even had specific rules for how leaders were expected to treat employees.

At the same time, that company maintained a constant focus on serving customers, while driving top-line sales, controlling expenses, and achieving bottom-line profitability. The CEO believed you can treat employees well and still have aggressive performance standards; he proved the two go hand in hand.

Achieving success begins with a good strategy, but your ultimate success or failure as a leader will still depend upon how well your team of empowered employees executes your strategy.

That company's leaders focused on leveraging the knowledge, skills, and abilities of employees by tapping into and harnessing their intellectual horsepower. In that positive environment, I saw average people performing at above-average levels. I experienced individual hourly employees coming up with great ideas that were implemented across the entire organization. I saw employees take the initiative to control company expenses while going out of their way to provide knock-your-socks-off service to customers. Individual employees and teams took ownership of business results as if they were business owners.

As an example, I saw teams of empowered hourly employees meeting unsupervised in closed-door conference rooms, developing solutions to complex organizational problems. At the end of the day, the employees would walk out of those meetings having developed practical solutions that could be quickly, easily, and inexpensively implemented. The first time I personally experienced the power of employee empowerment, I was shocked and a bit awed at what a team of truly empowered employees could achieve. I saw first-hand the value of teams of employees creating synergistic results. It was any CEO's dream come true!

Effective leaders surround themselves with great people, empower them, and then give them all the support, resources, and freedom they need to do their jobs.

That company believed that every employee at any organizational level has the capacity to step up and be a leader under the right circumstances. They also believed that if you take care of employees, employees will take care of the customers, and the bottom-line results will be there. As leaders, they lived by the philosophy of *employees first, customer service second, and sales and profits third*. With that employee engagement philosophy, the employees enthusiastically focused on providing outstanding customer service.

Your company can choose to adopt an employee-centered cultural philosophy that also maintains a focus on bottom-line results by teaching your entire leadership team to put the needs of employees ahead of all else. As an individual, you can choose to personally adopt the traits and behaviors of an employee-focused leader, even if your company won't. It's a simple decision you can make to change your personal leadership style.

VALUING EMPLOYEES

An effective leader's first job is to look out for the best interests of the employees on his or her team. In that context, you might say leadership is a form of *employee ambassadorship* on the front line. If you think about it, all organizational leaders should be required to act as ambassadors representing the interests of their organization's most important internal asset and constituency, its own employees. After all, the employees drive the business forward. They are the ones in contact with customers every day—solving problems, generating sales, controlling expenses, and creating company profits. When employees feel as though they are viewed as an important part of organizational success, their morale, creativity, and productivity increase. That's the secret to how to get average people to perform at above-average levels!

Take a moment and think about the leaders for whom you've worked over the years. *How many of them made you feel like they really cared about you and your career interests?* I am willing to bet you have experienced the same kind of fanatically bottom-line and profit-focused leadership that I did. I wonder how much more might have been accomplished if the leadership's focus and priority had been placed on training, rewarding, and recognizing teams and individual employees. Improving employee engagement is actually an easy problem to fix and is a worthwhile, high-impact business opportunity that can create a competitive advantage for your organization in the marketplace. For this reason alone, I am surprised more top executives don't see the value and the power of putting employees first, customer service second, and sales and profits third.

The truth is, *if you take care of your employees first, your employees will be motivated to take care of the business and your customers, generating outstanding top-line sales and remarkable bottom-line profits!* If you don't agree with that statement, think about it this way. If a supervisor doesn't show up for work today, the work will still get done, but if the employees don't show up, nothing gets done! Plain and simple, employees are the most important asset of any business.

Employees today expect, and maybe even demand, a more participative, shared decision-making style from their leaders.

Anyone in a leadership capacity can make the same choice that I did to put the needs of employees ahead of their own. All it takes is a commitment to be more concerned about supporting the needs of the people you work with and around. When you do, you'll discover you've become the kind of leader that employees willingly and enthusiastically choose to follow. You'll also unleash the withheld human potential of your entire team.

Once you get your leadership and cultural philosophies focused properly on employee engagement, everything else will fall into place. But until you do, getting results through people may continue to be a struggle.

EMPLOYEES MAKE THE DIFFERENCE

Changes in the way people are being led are transforming small and large organizations alike. In the twenty-first century, employee-centered leadership has become more common as companies have decided to abandon traditional command-and-control styles of leadership in favor of a participative approach to leading employees. To that point, great employee-oriented company cultures are common-place at companies such as Southwest Airlines, Virgin Group, REI, Chick-fil-A, Wegmans, Twitter, Edelman, Google, Chevron, P&G, Nike, Apple, and USAA.

Employees want to work for a compassionate leader who is trustworthy, respectful, fair, depend-able, collaborative, genuine, honest, appreciative, and responsive!

By focusing on their employees, these companies improve employee engagement and retention and customer service. The fact is, when leaders use a positive and partici-pative approach, employees are happier, more satisfied, and more productive. Not surprisingly, employee satisfaction enhances customer satisfaction, which in turn improves customer loyalty. By focusing on employee engagement, company leaders create a win-win scenario for employees, customers, and the company!

Today's job applicants search the internet for reviews of companies to find the best places to work. They read what current employees are saying about working there. They also read what prior employees, who have moved on, are saying. Companies have nowhere to hide from their leadership and cultural practices. When potential job applicants read these reviews, word gets around, and the best prospective new employees only seek out companies with the best reputations while avoiding the others.

By focusing on their own employees, companies create a positive perception in the employment marketplace. Putting employees first allows the great companies mentioned above to attract great talent, retain their existing teams, and motivate everyone to achieve company goals. The good news is, any company can do the same thing simply by setting new standards for employee engagement, training leaders to be more effective in their interactions with employees, and adopting an employee-centered culture.

An awareness of the complexity of engaging today's multigenerational, highly diverse employees is one of the key drivers behind companies changing the way they lead. It is important to note that lots of organizations and leaders are already practicing this style of leadership; some may be your direct competitors. If they are, they have created a significant competitive advantage over companies like yours that have been slow to adapt and change.

One of the reasons some CEOs and CFOs have been hesitant to even consider putting their employees' needs first is the misconception that focusing on people will dilute and lessen the performance of the top-line and bottom-line strategies of the business. Nothing could be further from the actual truth. **An employee-focused company culture does not take away an employee's accountability or responsibility for performing their regular job duties or for achieving the goals set by the company**. In fact, the focus on outstanding sales and service is actually enhanced when leaders place more value on people. It stands to reason that when employees feel valued, they dedicate themselves even more to their work, and experience has shown they produce even better work and results.

Adopting an employee-centered culture goes hand in hand with all your existing business strategies. They are not mutually exclusive; you will not lose momentum within your current objectives by shifting your culture. You can maintain a positive focus on your employees while simultaneously focusing your entire team on the same key performance indicators and key productivity and business initiatives as before. You will also continue to maintain a focus on the core vision and strategies that have historically driven your company's success. Examples of those specific company drivers might include:

Customer-Driven	*Sales-Driven*
R&D-Driven	*Market-Driven*
Technology-Driven	*Quality-Driven*
Competition-Driven	*Data-Driven*
Profit-Driven	*Marketing-Driven*
Merchandise-Driven	*Expense-Driven*
Supply Chain-Driven	*Price-Driven*
Innovation-Driven	

As an example, your organization can be a *customer-driven company with an employee-centered culture or an R&D-driven company with an employee-centered culture*, and so on.

The point is that your specific business driver(s) and any other strategic initiatives continue to remain front and center on your business agenda, translated into performance standards for your executives, managers, supervisors, and employees. The only thing that really changes is your forward-thinking approach to leading people and the focus of your company culture.

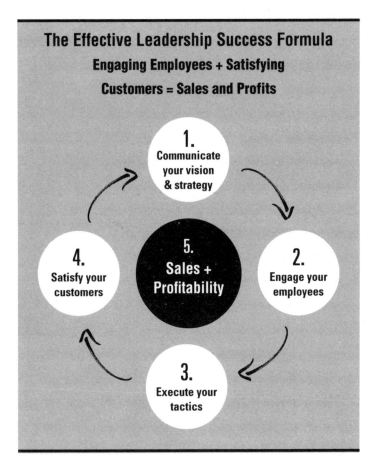

Companies with cultures that focus on *putting employees first, customers second, and sales/profits third* have discovered the secret to turning the power of people into a long-term competitive advantage. As a result, everybody wins: employees, management, customers, suppliers, and other stakeholders.

Not surprisingly, the leaders at companies like these always seem to have well-trained and highly motivated people on their bench ready, willing, and able to assume more responsible jobs as promotional opportunities become available. They have the ability to proliferate their employee-focused culture and outstanding customer service by promoting their own crop of well-trained, effective, people-focused leaders from within.

Unfortunately, one of the most daunting challenges to adopting an employee-centered culture in many organizations is overcoming the fixed beliefs of the current leadership team. From the top down, executives, managers, and supervisors may be resistant to change, preferring to continue leading from a position of power and authority. That flies in the face of employee-centered leadership, which uses a shared, more collaborative approach to making team decisions. That kind of major systemic cultural change can be difficult for an organization's leaders to swallow, but it can and should be done, because the short-term and long-term benefits are truly outstanding.

Putting the needs of employees ahead of everything

else—by creating an employee-centered culture—might just be the missing ingredient you have been looking for to complete your company's success formula. Unfortunately, cultural change will not occur naturally. Company executives must make a conscious decision to refocus company leaders and resources on creating an environment within which employees can thrive. That requires placing a long-term bet on the power of people today that will pay off handsomely in improved and ongoing company success in the future.

EFFECTIVE LEADERSHIP/EMPLOYEE ENGAGEMENT CHECKLIST

❑ Treat people the same way you would expect to be treated.

❑ Establish guidelines for how employees are to treat one another.

❑ Spend time interacting with employees one-on-one.

❑ Make yourself easily accessible to employees.

❑ Always have integrity and maintain confidentiality.

❑ Hold people accountable for the commitments they make to you.

❑ Seek input from employees when you are making decisions impacting them.

❑ Share your knowledge by teaching employees new skills.

❑ Admit your mistakes and take full responsibility for your actions.

❑ Follow the rules the same way you expect others to follow them.

- ❏ Make keeping employees informed a daily priority.
- ❏ Delegate all the responsibility and authority employees need to succeed.
- ❏ Stop what you are doing to sincerely listen to what others are saying to you.
- ❏ Provide periodic performance updates to your individual team members.
- ❏ Ask employees for their ideas and help to solve work-related problems.
- ❏ Sincerely recognize employee accomplishments as they happen.
- ❏ Spend time out of your office working directly with employees.
- ❏ Take the time to really get to know the people you work with.
- ❏ Set individual and team "stretch" goals, with employee input.
- ❏ Empathetically listen and respond to employees who have personal problems.
- ❏ Always be consistent and fair in your dealings with all employees.

- ❑ Project loyalty and commitment to your organization for all to see.
- ❑ Give constructive feedback and address problems in a timely manner.
- ❑ Set a good example by embracing organizational changes.
- ❑ Treat everyone with the respect and dignity they deserve.
- ❑ Develop the talents of employees via a combination of coaching and mentorship.
- ❑ Make certain new employees receive a thorough cultural and job orientation.
- ❑ Hire great people who have the potential to one day be your boss.

DIVERSE AND MULTIGENERATIONAL EMPLOYEES

FOR THE PAST SEVERAL decades, the beliefs, values, and expectations of the people in the workforce have been constantly changing and evolving. There is no reason to believe that trend won't continue into the future. Consider the fact that employees today are more entrepreneurial minded, they're more tech-savvy, and they want their opinions to be seriously considered when decisions impacting them are being made. Employees expect, and maybe even demand, a more participative, shared decision-making style from their company leaders.

Adding to the challenge of leading multigenerational employees are the differences in the way people think and behave based on race, gender, ethnicity, religion, sex, disability, and/or sexual orientation.

U.S. Workforce Composition

The U.S. workforce is composed of 53 percent men and 47 percent women, according to the United States Bureau of Labor Statistics (2015).[2] Undoubtedly, the workforce is also becoming more diverse as people of color make up 37 percent of today's employees. Breaking it down by race and ethnicity, approximately 63 percent of the workforce is non-Hispanic white; 16 percent is Hispanic; 12 percent is African American; 6 percent is Asian; and 3 percent do not identify with any of these racial or ethnic categories.

A Robert Half survey revealed that 72 percent of managers find it challenging to manage diverse teams composed of members of different generations.[3] This challenge is particularly evident for younger-generation leaders who are put in the position of managing Baby Boomers in the workforce. On the other hand, more tenured managers and supervisors, who are accustomed to managing Baby Boomers, have found they must modify their approach when working with a diverse and multigenerational workforce composed of a mixture of Baby Boomers and Generation X, Y, and in the near future, Gen Z employees.

Diversity Versus Inclusion Defined

Inclusion is a perception, feeling, or belief on the part of an employee or group of employees that they are valued, respected, and supported by the company's leaders as well as by their fellow employees. Inclusion is about respecting what each person brings to the workplace, building teamwork, and helping each individual achieve their full potential. In simple terms, diversity is the mix of people in the work group who are from different backgrounds, races, ethnicities, sexual orientations, genders, and ages; inclusion is getting that mix of people to work together productively and seamlessly.

FOUR GENERATIONS

Here are brief descriptions of the four generations of workers in today's workforce, along with some insights about each.

The Silent Generation, or Greatest Generation, born between 1925–1945, is the fifth generation, but because so few are still employed, and the majority are already retired, they will not be focused upon in this book.

BABY BOOMERS

Baby Boomers (born 1946–1964), also known as Boomers and the Post-War Generation, are the generation born during the post–World War II baby boom. They experienced economic prosperity throughout their lives primarily due to higher education, government subsidies, rising home prices, and advances in technology. Many Baby Boomers are on the brink of retirement or already there. By 2020, this generation will only represent 22 percent of the total working population.[4] Examples of Baby Boomers include Samuel L. Jackson, Hillary Clinton, Billy Joel, and Bill Gates.

Insights

▶ The Post-War Generation was the first generation to reject traditional values and instead embrace social changes.

▶ Baby Boomers value competition and enjoy competing with their peers, as long as they win.

▶ They were the originators of the live-to-work workaholic trend.

▶ The Post-War Generation has always viewed

success in their job as their ticket to the next level of success in life, even if that success throws off their own work-life balance.

▶ Baby Boomers witnessed the birth of rock and roll, the civil rights movement, and the beginnings of space exploration. They are the most affluent generation in the history of the world. According to a McKinsey Global Institute report, Boomers have collectively earned $3.7 trillion, more than twice as much as the $1.6 trillion that members of the Silent Generation did at the same age.[5]

▶ Baby Boomers are a particularly loyal generation, and they will be the last to value working for a single employer for an entire career.

▶ Boomers are every organization's go-to know-how experts who employees from other generations learn from. They are motivated by the chance to share their expertise with other workers.

▶ Many top executives and senior-level managers are Baby Boomers.

GEN X

Generation X (born 1965–1980), also known as Gen X, were born in the generation right after the Baby Boomers and just before the Millennials. The lives of Gen X employees were shaped by the Vietnam War, the fall of the Berlin Wall, and the end of the Cold War. Compared to previous generations, Gen X employees are more open to diversity, having learned to embrace differences such as religion, sexual orientation, gender, class, disability, age, race, and ethnicity. Michael Dell, Jennifer Lopez, and Paul Ryan are Gen Xers.

Insights

- Unlike the Baby Boomers, Generation Xers don't live to work; they work to live.
- Gen Xers are fun-loving and take a *work hard and play hard* approach to life.
- Gen Xers are ambitious and eager to learn new skills, but they like to accomplish things on their own terms.
- Although they are the most highly educated generation, they still experience high unemployment and underemployment.[6]

- ▶ Fear of missing out (FOMO) seems to be the common denominator for this constantly technologically connected generation.

- ▶ Generation Xers value jobs, leaders, and companies that offer them freedom and responsibility.

- ▶ As managers, they generally embrace a hands-off management philosophy.

- ▶ They are less committed to a single employer; as a result, they expect to periodically change jobs and companies, and they often do.

GEN Y

Generation Y (born 1981–2000), employees also referred to as Millennials or Gen Y, were born in the years immediately following Generation X. Gen Yers has been shaped by the technological revolution that occurred throughout their lifetimes. Gen Y grew up with technology, so they are masters of its cutting-edge forms. Many are equipped with the latest technology such as iPhones, laptops, game consoles, smartphones, and tablets. With Baby Boomer parents, who worked hard to earn a living, as their example, Gen Y employees prefer a work-life balance. Kate Middleton, Usain Bolt, Mark Zuckerberg, and Justin Timberlake are from Generation Y.

According to Sarah Sladek, founder of XYZ University and author of the book, *Knowing Y: Engaging the Next Generation Now*, this tech-savvy, globally minded generation isn't joining, buying, networking, learning, or engaging like other generations. Sladek believes Gen Y is different from other generations. She uses these facts to make her point:[7]

- ▶ 92 percent believe that business success should be measured by more than profit.
- ▶ 80 percent prefer on-the-spot recognition over formal reviews.
- ▶ 61 percent feel personally responsible to make a difference in the world.
- ▶ 50 percent want to start their own business or have already done so.
- ▶ Two years is their average employment tenure.

Insights

- ▶ Many of this generation live with their parents, due to difficulties reaching financial independence, and many are saddled with large college loans.

▶ Many Gen Yers are actively pursuing corporate careers, while at the same time, they are passionate about making some kind of difference in the world around them.

▶ Making $40,000 annually and being happy at their job is far more appealing to Gen Yers than making $80,000 annually and being miserable. They learned this lesson by watching their parents and other miserable Baby Boomers who continued to work at jobs they detested.

▶ Creativity and speedy communication are the norm for this generation due to mastery of instant messaging, blogging, microblogging, podcasting, social networking, and photo and video sharing.

▶ Confident, entrepreneurial minded, and fearless, they don't feel they need prerequisite experience because they have always been able to solve problems instantaneously via YouTube and the internet. Short on patience, they want everything now.

▶ The attitude that they can do anything makes them oblivious to limitations, barriers, and obstructions.

▶ They value flexible work schedules, opportunities to travel the world, and a good work-life balance.

▸ Gen Yers share the Gen X fear of missing out (FOMO), so they remain online and connected constantly.

▸ They prefer to work for a socially responsible employer that shares their values.

▸ Their parents taught them not to trust their employer, so they tend to look out for themselves. Many are entrepreneurs, consultants, and business owners.

According to MillennialMarketing.com, Gen Yers:[8]

✓ value **family**, **personal connection**, and **loyalty**.

✓ seek out the **genuine** and are repulsed by the **phony**.

✓ are famously **optimistic** and believe in the possibility of **change**.

✓ advocate for the **environment** and **social justice**.

✓ treasure **tolerance** and **diversity**, **teamwork** and **balance**.

✓ seek **spirituality** and are open to the possibility of the divine.

GEN Z

Generation Z (born 2001–2020), also known as Gen Z, the Net Generation, iGeneration, Centennials, Post-Millennials, Plurals, or the Homeland Generation, are the offspring of Generation X and Generation Y parents. They are about to begin entering the workforce. They are growing up with technology, and the older members of Gen Z are already prolific users of social media. It is a little early to predict with any certainty what they will expect in the work world. Sasha Obama, Maddie Ziegler, and Romeo Beckham are all from the Net Generation.

Insights

- ▶ Generation Z is the first generation to be raised in the era of smartphones. For Gen Z, owning and using a smartphone will be quite normal from an early age.
- ▶ The majority of this generation is and will be nonwhite. That is the first time this has occurred in United States history.
- ▶ The vast majority were not even born when 9/11 took place, but their parents and teachers have made the event a part of their lives.

- ▶ They grew up in a world of terrorist acts, fear, and insecurities.

- ▶ The Great Recession caused a weak economy and lack of jobs that affected both their parents and them.

- ▶ They learned from their parents not to trust an employer to look out for them, so they are entrepreneurial minded.

- ▶ They accept and embrace rapid change as a normal part of life.

MULTIGENERATIONAL EMPLOYEE ENGAGEMENT

Employees today are driven by open communication, a great company culture, involvement with causes, and achieving purpose and personal fulfillment. Leaders need to be aware that Generation X and Y employees will quit a job simply to find a new one at a new company working for a supervisor who will be more in tune with their values.

You can find proof of this in some of your own employee files. Dig out some Generation X and Y employees' personnel files, and take a look at their résumés or job applications. You'll probably notice that the job they hold at your company is one of a string of jobs. You may find examples of employees who have had three, five, or more different jobs (if they listed them all) before they reached the age of thirty! There is no reason to believe that job-changing mentality is going to alter as employees get older, especially if the engagement strategies of companies remain the same.

The important message here is that company executives, managers, and supervisors (many of whom are Baby Boomers) are the ones who need to adapt and change—or risk negative consequences. The strategy of leading people the same old way you have always led them won't deliver the same old results. Achieving different and even better results requires a new and more innovative approach to engaging and leading people. Leaders must adapt and change—or fail. It's as simple as that.

To succeed as a leader today requires understanding the nuances of leading a diverse group of employees who come from different racial and ethnic backgrounds, sexual orientations, religions, genders, disabilities, and generations and whose engagement levels may vary based on the differences in how they were socialized growing up. One-size-fits-all leadership isn't nearly as effective as tailoring your leadership style to meet the individual needs of today's highly diverse and multigenerational workforce.

Five Generations of Workers[9]

SILENT The Greatest Generation	1925 to 1945	Loyalty, Respect for Authority, Discipline, Adherence to Rules	1%
BABY BOOMERS The Post-War Generation	1946 to 1964	Optimism, Innovation, Achievement, Individualism	22%
GENERATION X Gen X	1965 to 1980	Autonomy, Productivity, Recognition, Adaptability	20%
GENERATION Y Millennials	1981 to 2000	Self-Expression, Change Is Good, Resilience, Global Awareness, Connectivity	50%
GENERATION Z Next Generation	2001 to 2020	Technical Knowledge, Fast Pace, Social Connection, Creativity, Collaboration	7%

IIIIIIIIIIIIIIIIIIIIIIIII

Engaging your employees has been, is, and always will be the best strategy for creating a sustainable competitive advantage in the marketplace.

IIIIIIIIIIIIIIIIIIIIIIIII

COMPANIES LARGE AND SMALL have waged the battle for the hearts, hands, and minds of employees for decades—and for good reason. The triple whammy resulting from top-line revenue reduction has resulted in:

1. Expenses spiraling out of control
2. Erosion of bottom-line profitability
3. Layoffs of staff members

The circumstances behind this reality are many and varied, including global competition, the introduction of new technologies, antiquated products, more agile competitors, and simply a failure to adapt and change.

As a leader, this isn't news to you. You've watched as this phenomenon has unfolded around you for as long as you've been in business. Employees around the globe have also taken notice. Keep in mind that the employees who have been laid off or downsized, as well as those who survived the cutbacks, have experienced the collateral damage. Those traumatic experiences have changed the career reality of all employees and forever changed how they view loyalty and the work world. That attitude has become the new normal!

As a result, companies and leaders are facing an employee attraction, retention, and motivation crisis. Whether we care to admit it or not, company leaders and employees are facing a new employment reality, and employee engagement is at an unacceptable level.

In fact, the term *employee loyalty* has long been an example of an oxymoron. That's because employees have been conditioned to look out for themselves due to the callous employment practices and harsh leadership prevalent in so many organizations. Many employees learned these lessons the hard way—by watching their parents go through periods of unemployment, as well as a series of unplanned and forced job changes, while they were growing

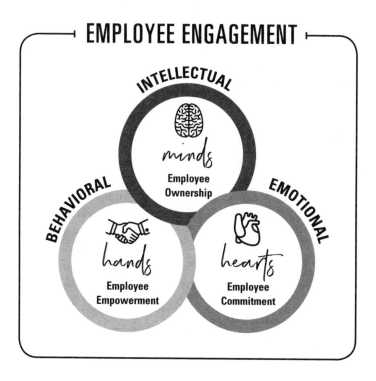

up. Also keep in mind that many employees have already experienced the emotional distress of staff reductions or callous leadership.

As an HR executive, I have experienced the collateral damage of decreasing employee loyalty firsthand. For many of your current employees, working for your company may only be a temporary stop on their career journey, one of many jobs that will show up on their résumés in the years to come.

If you conducted exit interviews, departing employees would tell you different reasons for their decision to leave. Some may say they didn't feel respected by their supervisor, or in reverse, they didn't respect their boss. Others may tell you their personal values didn't align with those of the company. Still others may say their personal career goals were out of alignment with the expectations of the organization.

If you are willing to listen to those who are leaving your employment, you will actually gain an awareness and a better understanding of the concerns, feelings, and expectations of many of the employees who are still working for you!

It's obvious from these insights that employees feel their current company and their current supervisor aren't recognizing, appreciating, and valuing them and their contributions. More often than not, when employees have had enough, they don't quit because they dislike their jobs; they quit to go find a better boss and a better company.

The reasons behind this breakdown in employee loyalty and commitment (from an employee's standpoint) become clear when you study the three levels of employee engagement.

1. **Fully Engaged**: In days gone by, employees and companies were unquestionably loyal to one another; that is just the way it was. Whether you liked your supervisor and company or not, if you had a good job, you stayed in it and with the same employer until you retired. Employees were unquestionably committed, *fully engaged*, and loyal to their employer for life. I characterize an employee with that level of commitment and engagement as having *both feet in*. Times have changed, and the days when employees could expect *cradle-to-grave* employment with the same company are far behind us.

2. **Partially Engaged**: It seems the strategy embraced by many workers today is to remain gainfully employed and continue to do an acceptable job, while constantly keeping an eye out for a perceived better career opportunity. Those employees are only *partially engaged*. I call this new employee job

strategy *straddling the line*, with a commitment or engagement level characterized by always having *one foot in and one foot out*.

3. **Totally Disengaged**: It gets worse. Today, there are employees at all levels of organizations—including executives, managers, supervisors, and frontline employees—who are no longer committed to their employer and their job, yet they still come to work every day. Some are afraid to look for new opportunities, so they show up, go through the motions, and continue to collect a paycheck. They are *totally disengaged*, doing just enough to keep from getting fired, but little more than that. I characterize the psychological commitment or engagement level of this kind of employee as having *both feet out*.

The Employee Engagement Levels as Reported in a 2017 Gallup Poll:[10]

DISENGAGED
16 PERCENT

FULLY ENGAGED
33 PERCENT

ENGAGEMENT

PARTIALLY ENGAGED
51 PERCENT

How can companies expect to prosper with so many unhappy, partially engaged, and totally disengaged employees? From a people leadership standpoint, the employee engagement picture looks awfully bleak. *Based on what you've just read, what level of engagement do your employees have for the work they do for you? Are they totally committed and fully engaged with both feet in, do they straddle the commitment line, partially engaged, with one foot in and one foot out, or are they totally disengaged with both feet out?*

You may struggle with the answer to whether your employees are truly engaged in their work. You may decide that some are engaged and some aren't, and some you're just not sure about. You may even believe there is nothing to worry about, because your team measures comparably to the average engagement statistics previously listed. That way of thinking is unacceptable and will only worsen your problems with employee engagement. You owe it to your organization and to your employees to make a commitment to improve. Though you may not think it's possible, your ultimate goal must be 100 percent employee engagement. You want everyone to come to work each day with both feet in. As an effective leader, you must approach employees each day with that goal in mind.

iiiiiiiiiiiiiiiiiiiiiiiiiiiiii

Orientation or onboarding of new hires is the critical initial and ongoing process of acclimating employees to the policies, practices, procedures, and culture of the organization.

iiiiiiiiiiiiiiiiiiiiiiiiiiiiii

I hate to be the bearer of bad news, but most employee disengagement can be attributed directly to the way people are being led. It's called poor or ineffective leadership. Unfortunately, most top leaders were taught a different style of old-school leadership that put profits first and people second. Many companies seem to gravitate toward leaders who are bottom-line-focused taskmasters, who are rewarded for hitting the numbers while simultaneously being really tough on people.

Some leaders assume that employees don't want to do a good job and that employees wouldn't willingly do the work on their own without being managed by their boss. However, employees don't like to be managed, and they don't respond well to an overbearing, dictatorial, and negative style of leadership. In fact, when people are managed, prodded, and pushed, job performance actually suffers, and performance is withheld. That's why *employee engagement* has become one of the major concerns of top leaders in companies both small and large across industries.

In 2016, the Society for Human Resource Management (SHRM) conducted an employee job satisfaction and engagement survey. In that survey, employees were asked more than forty job-satisfaction opinion questions about different aspects of their jobs. Fourteen of those questions are summarized in the following chart.[11]

SOURCE: SHRM 2016	A	B	Δ
JOB SATISFACTION CATEGORY	**VERY IMPORTANT**	**VERY SATISFIED**	**DIFFERENCE BETWEEN A AND B**
Compensation/pay	63%	23%	40%
Respectful treatment of employees	67%	31%	36%
Trust between employees and top executives	55%	27%	28%
Job security	58%	32%	26%
Job advancement	47%	24%	23%
Communication from executives to employees	48%	25%	23%
Employee recognition	48%	26%	22%
Communication of company goals and strategy	45%	24%	21%
Opportunities to use skill/abilities	55%	37%	18%
Career development opportunities	39%	21%	18%
Overall corporate culture	44%	28%	16%

SOURCE: SHRM 2016	A	B	Δ
JOB SATISFACTION CATEGORY	VERY IMPORTANT	VERY SATISFIED	DIFFERENCE BETWEEN A AND B
The work itself	48%	34%	14%
Relationship with immediate supervisor	53%	40%	13%
Respect for employee's ideas	49%	37%	12%

To clarify the meaning of the data in the table, here is an example. For the category *communication from executives to employees*, 48 percent of surveyed employees rated it very important, yet only 25 percent reported they were very satisfied with level of communication from executives. That difference between "very important" and "very satisfied" in this example is 23 percent. In fact, in all the job-satisfaction categories that were rated by employees as "very important," there is a corresponding rating for "very satisfied" that is lower by double digits. That means that in all the job-satisfaction categories listed, the company and its leaders are not meeting the expectations of their own employees. You can identify and calibrate employee perceptions of your company, its leaders, and their jobs via your own employee opinion survey.

Remember that the real value of the survey is in actually sitting down with employees in a group meeting to discuss their feelings and the reasoning behind their survey results. The ultimate short- and long-term goal of surveying employee opinions is the proactive development of a strategy for resolving any problems identified.

TOP EXECUTIVES MUST INITIATE CHANGE

To be clear, an employee engagement strategy is not an initiative that can be successfully driven and implemented by the HR department. It is a company and cultural initiative that is owned by the CEO and top executive team and driven downward to the frontline supervisors. It requires the communication of specific actions, beliefs, competencies, and values. Once ABCs are established, employee-focused leadership will become an integral part of the cultural DNA of the organization and all its leaders. If individual executives, managers, or supervisors don't like this approach or disagree with it, they have no choice but to adapt to it, embrace it, or leave. That's how important engaging employees is to organizational success going forward.

Engaging your employees has been, is, and always will

be the best strategy for creating a sustainable competitive advantage in the marketplace.

Let's face it. Your employees are the primary interface between your company and your customers. They are the ones who sell your products and services. Following that logic, your employees make the difference between the success and the failure of your enterprise. For this reason, lack of employee engagement is a problem companies must address and solve in order to remain relevant, competitive, and successful.

So the question is: *What can company leaders do to improve employee engagement?* Lore International Institute conducted a research study published in 2006 to determine the answer to that question by asking employees what they really want and expect from their manager or supervisor.[12] Here are the findings of that research:

- ▶ **Honesty**: 91.5 percent want honesty and integrity from their manager.
- ▶ **Fairness**: 89.2 percent want their manager to be fair and to hold everyone accountable for the same standards.
- ▶ **Trust**: 86.7 percent want to trust and be trusted by their manager.

- ► **Respect**: 84.7 percent want to respect and be respected by their manager.
- ► **Dependability**: 81.2 percent want to be able to count on their manager.
- ► **Collaboration**: 77.4 percent want to be a part of their manager's team and be asked to contribute ideas and solutions.
- ► **Genuineness**: 76.2 percent want their manager to be a genuine person.
- ► **Appreciation**: 74.4 percent want their manager to appreciate them for who they are and what they do.
- ► **Responsiveness**: 73.9 percent want their manager to listen, understand, and respond.

While it's important to know what your employees need, it is just as vital to understand what they don't want from their manager. Among Lore International Institute's somewhat surprising findings:

- ► **Friendship**: Only 3 percent want their manager to be a friend. As in parenting, it's more important to be a leader, mentor, and example than a buddy.

▶ **Conversation**: Only 14 percent want to have interesting conversations with their manager.

▶ **TLC**: Only 24 percent say they want their manager to "care for them." That doesn't mean you have to be cold and detached, but most employees aren't looking for a best friend in their boss.

▶ **Emotional support**: Only 25 percent want emotional support from their manager. Employees typically look for that among coworkers rather than from a boss.

▶ **Cheerfulness**: Only 28 percent want a cheerful or happy manager. They'd rather respect you than like you.

Based on the research results, employees want to work for a compassionate leader, one who is trustworthy, respectful, fair, dependable, collaborative, genuine, honest, appreciative, and responsive.[13] That is very good news, because it plays to the strengths of effective leaders. It helps provide a clear path to what an individual leader—as well as a leadership team—can do proactively and should be doing to address the employee engagement problem.

Your company is not the only one struggling with the

challenges of attracting new employees, retaining existing staff, and motivating your current team. Your competitors are experiencing similar challenges. You can bet your
competition is actively pursuing employee engagement
solutions that can give them a leg up on companies like
yours. Knowing that, your company's leaders can gain a
competitive edge by proactively establishing your own
employee-centered culture and focusing on engaging your
own employees, starting today.

The choice is up to you. The way you lead going forward
can transform your employees into your company's greatest asset or make them your company's biggest liability.
The battle to engage the hearts and minds and hands of
your current and future employees can be won by engaging
them on an intellectual, behavioral, and emotional level.
Employee engagement is a battle that must be waged, and
it must be won. Your success as a leader and the long-term
viability of your company depend on it.

EMPLOYEES FIRST, CUSTOMERS SECOND, AND PROFITS THIRD TO IMPROVE SALES, SERVICE, AND PROFITABILITY

Employees who are fully engaged and totally committed can be the difference between a company leading an industry versus lagging behind its competitors.

EMPLOYEE ENGAGEMENT BUILDS EMPLOYEE morale as it simultaneously drives top-line sales-revenue growth and bottom-line profitability, while enhancing customer relations. It almost sounds too good to be true, doesn't it?

In the Towers Watson (now Willis Towers Watson) 2014 Global Workforce Study, employees reported having manager/employee engagement expectations that weren't being met. The survey states:

> **After decades of emphasizing employees' responsibility to know the customers' needs and meet them, many employees are starting to expect the same from**

**their employer. Seventy percent of employees agree
that their organization should understand employees
to the same degree that employees are expected to
understand customers. However, fewer than half (43
percent of employees) report having an employer
that understands them in this way. Employees who
feel their organization is effective in these areas are
significantly more likely to be highly engaged than
those who do not.[14]**

As reported in the Global Workforce Study, focusing
on employee engagement can be a transformational strategy for your organization that will change the way leaders
focus on achieving goals. By shifting their focus from the
goals themselves to the employees responsible for achieving
the goals, leaders will improve employee engagement and
commitment, which will ultimately lead to higher levels of
goal achievement.

||||||||||||||||||||||||||||||

Leaders are responsible for creating a work environment that is so positive that employees willingly unleash their full potential.

||||||||||||||||||||||||||||||

Focusing on employees isn't about paying people more money as an inducement to drive increased productivity. Financial incentives alone aren't the key to employee job satisfaction, morale, or improved productivity anyway. The answer is for leaders to create an employee-centered work culture that is so caring, supportive, and participative that employees want to do a good job. They will enjoy coming to work every day, and they will choose to stay with the company. That renewed employee enthusiasm and commitment can't help but spill over into the quality of service you provide to your customers.

When a company creates a positive work environment, employees will actually like their jobs more, because they are happier and more satisfied. That's because engaged employees feel better about themselves, their company leaders, and their company. Though this method of leadership may challenge your beliefs about how you lead a team, it's hard to argue with the facts in the following research:

Happiness = Productivity and Employee Satisfaction

A 2015 Happiness and Productivity study by economists at the University of Warwick, UK, found that worker happiness led to a 12 percent spike in productivity, while unhappy workers proved 10 percent less productive.[15] As the research team put it, "We find that human happiness has large and positive causal effects on productivity."[16] Professor Andrew Oswald, one of three researchers who led the study, said companies that invest in employee support and satisfaction tend to succeed in generating happier workers. At Google, employee satisfaction rose 37 percent as a result of those initiatives![17]

The University of Warwick study makes a strong business case for adopting the principles of employee-focused leadership.

The takeaways from this study are:

▸ If you support your employees with strong and consistent leadership values, your employees will be happier, more satisfied, and more productive workers.

▸ Happy and satisfied employees provide better customer service, making customers more satisfied, which generates higher sales and profits.

▸ The fact that happy employees are more productive employees is the best *business case* argument of all for adopting employee-focused leadership values and philosophies.

EMPLOYEE POTENTIAL

As an HR executive, I worked at both small and large companies that struggled with having enough high-performing and high-potential employees ready as promotional opportunities became available. I found many of our employees weren't willing to make the personal sacrifices required to prepare in advance for promotions. The employees still expected to get promoted, before they were ready, believing they would develop the skills and gain the knowledge required to succeed once they were in the new role.

The scenario I just described is an example of intentionally *withheld human potential*. When I say withheld potential, what I mean is every manager and employee has within them the ability to perform at levels of productivity 10 percent, 15 percent, or even more above their current level of performance. In addition, teams in most organizations never achieve at a level that creates true synergy. The combined efforts of individual team members fall short of generating synergistic results. This is not surprising when the 2017 State of the American Workplace Gallup report revealed 67 percent of employees are only partially engaged or totally disengaged in their work.[18] That is an incredible amount of withheld human potential. It is a problem worth solving, and the good news is that with the right people strategy, it can be solved.

‖‖‖‖‖‖‖‖‖‖‖‖‖‖‖‖‖

Every manager and employee can perform at levels 10 percent, 15 percent, or even more beyond their current level of performance.

‖‖‖‖‖‖‖‖‖‖‖‖‖‖‖‖‖

What if I told you that your organization could unlock that untapped potential in individuals and teams by establishing an employee-focused cultural philosophy?

It's true. You can draw out that untapped executive, management, and employee potential and achieve at levels you may have previously thought weren't possible. Change is difficult for employees—and for supervisors, managers, and executives as well—but it can be done. It all starts by making a commitment, starting at the top, by focusing on changing the way employees are *managed and led*.

As I close this chapter, I'd like to dispel a myth regarding putting your employees first. Some leaders mistakenly believe that sales, service, production, and profits will suffer as a result of implementing an employee-centered approach. That's simply not true. In an earlier chapter, I referenced many great companies that are achieving monumental success while embracing more effective employee-focused leadership practices. Some of them may even be your competitors!

Five Characteristics of Highly Engaged Employees

So what does an engaged employee look like? The reality is that employee engagement takes many different forms. Here are five examples of the behaviors of highly engaged employees.

1. **They Are Company Ambassadors**—They tell everybody they know how proud they are to work for your company and that it is a great place to work. They are the best recruiters of new employees. *They reinforce and build the company's reputational equity.*

2. **They Are Loyal**—Through thick and thin, engaged employees can be relied upon to help their company work through inevitable workplace challenges. When things happen that negatively impact employees, those engaged and highly loyal employees often remain the voice of reason. Many times, they are the ones who bring issues to the attention of managers so that positive and equitable solutions can be found. *They reinforce and build the company's long-term cultural equity.*

3. **They Are Brand Evangelists**—They enthusiastically tell their family, friends, and potential customers about your company's products and services, and they broadcast their beliefs and feelings across their social networks. *They reinforce and build the company's brand equity.*

4. **They Are Employee Mentors**—They willingly take new employees under their wing to ensure a smooth transition into the company. With or without management involvement, engaged employees proactively assist newly hired employees by answering questions, solving problems, and teaching them "what it takes to be successful here." *They reinforce and build the company's human resource equity.*

5. **They Are Driven to Succeed**—Engaged employees are driven to achieve their production, sales, and service goals. They provide superior internal and external customer service. They strive to perform to the best of their ability, and they lead by their own example. Their passion positively influences fellow employees as well as customers. *They reinforce and build the company's internal and external customer equity.*

||||||||||||||||||||||||||||||||

**Remember: the employees ultimately
decide whether or not you have what
it takes to be an effective leader!**

||||||||||||||||||||||||||||||||

EFFECTIVELY LEADING A DIVERSE and multigenerational workforce starts with adopting a set of values. There are several leadership values to choose from, including *supporting employees, valuing relationships, empowering employees, respecting people, inspiring trust, communicating values, and engaging employees.* These "people values" act as filters that a leader uses to shape his or her behaviors and decisions in interaction with people at home, at work, and out in the world. Of the values listed, three provide a solid foundation as core guiding principles for effective leaders: respecting people, inspiring trust, and supporting employees.

RESPECTING PEOPLE

Respect is showing admiration and deep regard for another individual. Not surprisingly, the desire to be treated with respect is at the top of every employee's (and manager's) list. As a leader, when you treat employees with respect, you send the message that you have high regard for the capabilities they bring to the workplace. You show that you respect others when you acknowledge their rights, opinions, ideas, wishes, experience, and competence.

INSPIRING TRUST

Building trust starts by getting to know every member of your team and developing strong interpersonal relationships. Once employees get to know who you are, they'll understand where you're coming from as a leader, making it less likely they will question your motives. Once employees trust you, more often than not, they will give you the benefit of the doubt, even when they may not personally agree with a decision you've made.

SUPPORTING EMPLOYEES

A leader supports employees by putting their needs first—supporting them as they work and focusing on their growth and development. It's all about keeping the focus on the employees and away from self.

Values-driven leadership is important. Leaders who are driven by a set of values are more apt to be open, honest communicators who serve as employee advocates. Acting as mentors, effective leaders routinely focus on the growth and development of employees, with a goal of developing future leaders for their organization. The best leaders work side by side with their employees as needed. Leading by example, effective leaders demonstrate the values, work ethic, and interpersonal skills expected from others. Not only do they give employees the responsibility, authority, and freedom to do their jobs, but they also have tolerance for the inevitable setbacks and failures.

The interesting thing about these core leadership values is that the determination of whether you are living up to them is not your call. You see, the people around you decide whether or not you are respectful, trustworthy, and supportive of employees. Your employees, your family, and your friends determine whether you are living up to those values. Through their observations of your words, deeds, and actions, they alone make the final determination of whether you have what it takes to be an effective twenty-first-century leader. Their perception of your effectiveness as a leader represents their reality, not yours!

Emulating an outstanding mentor is the fastest way to change your own leadership behavior. The best way to become a more effective leader is to watch leadership being practiced by an expert who you respect and admire. That is exactly what happened to me. I worked for a CEO who modeled the correct ABCs for all to see. I was sold on becoming a more effective leader of employees when I saw the reaction of the people around me to his caring leadership style and his sincere concern for them as people.

As he communicated, I watched him weave messages about providing outstanding customer service, maintaining productivity standards, controlling expenses, and remaining focused on bottom-line results. Everyone willingly bought into his strategies, quite honestly because he was so obviously concerned about them that they didn't want to let him down!

That CEO had discovered a great secret about human motivation. When people are emotionally invested in their own success and the success of the enterprise, they enthusiastically want to contribute whatever they can to achieving great results. Caring about them ignites a burning desire inside every employee to prove to their leader that his or her trust, caring, and belief in them are well founded!

To be clear, the creation of an employee-focused culture isn't a strategy that simply involves leaders acting in a *motivational or positive* way. It's not a speech or a single rah-rah, pump-'em-up rollout meeting. It is much more substantial than trying to inspire people through upbeat exhortations. Employee-centered leadership is not a *program du jour, a management fad, or a trendy new-wave management process*. It is not even a *management technique*. It is a long-term commitment to human relations by an organization committed to changing the way its leaders lead people.

Employee-centered leadership is defined as a leadership style that emphasizes interpersonal relationships, participatory decision-making, and employee support. For leaders, it requires a commitment to learning a new, different, and more effective approach to leading people.

In addition to the leader's motivation to lead, he or she must have an equally strong desire to support employees and put their needs first. To be effective, a leader must do everything they can to selflessly help, nurture, and support their employees to succeed. Such leaders become externally focused on the success of employees and the company, rather than solely on their own selfish goals.

Employee-Centered Leadership, Putting Employees First, and Employee Engagement Are:

- ✓ Converting the power of people into a sustainable competitive advantage.
- ✓ The most desirable state of the employer-employee relationship.
- ✓ About employee ownership of business results.
- ✓ Communicating to employees where the business is going and how they fit in.
- ✓ About organizational success, driven by committed employees.
- ✓ Empowering employees to serve internal and external customers.
- ✓ Recognizing and rewarding employee contributions.
- ✓ Inspiring everyone to willingly get behind business initiatives.

- ✓ An outcome of caring, listening, building trust, and empowering employees.
- ✓ About helping people reach their full potential.
- ✓ Impassioned leaders igniting the same level of passion in employees.
- ✓ Making employees feel appreciated so they want to stay and do a good job.
- ✓ Attracting, retaining, and motivating a high-performing work group.
- ✓ Leaders selflessly putting the needs of employees ahead of their own.
- ✓ A key indicator of effective leadership.

Typically, the managers and supervisors working closest to the employees are eager to adopt and practice *employee-first values*. That's because they can see and feel the benefits firsthand, as employees respond enthusiastically to their leader's employee-centered approach.

Every leader has the capacity to learn the human relations techniques necessary for engaging a diverse and multigenerational workforce. The process starts with a commitment to developing caring, mentoring, nurturing, and trust-based relationships. Most importantly, while building on those relationships, the leader and the team simultaneously maintain a focus on productivity, performance, and profitability. It truly is a situation in which everybody succeeds: the employees, the customers, the company, and the leader.

It is important to note that effective leaders think more about advancing and supporting the needs of the people around them than about their own needs. That type of selfless leadership is focused on helping employees achieve their goals. Effective leaders know that when their employees succeed, they will be successful as well.

When leaders focus on the success of all team members, every individual becomes more committed and even more motivated to perform at higher levels, resulting in team synergy. It's a win-win strategy that lifts people up while simultaneously raising the performance of the organization. In the final analysis, that in itself makes a fairly solid business case for adopting the principles of employee-centered leadership.

Five Things That Really Matter to Employees

An employee's perspective of what you can do to be a more effective leader
by Maranda G., Gen Y, Office Staff, Chicago

I. Leverage My Personal Talents
Do you really know what I am good at?

If you are a manager, it's a good idea to explore the strengths, weaknesses, skills, and abilities of all your current employees. You might be surprised to know what talented people you already have on your staff. Give people like me the chance to prove what I am capable of doing by entrusting me with more responsibility. I won't let you down.

II. Let Me Talk to You
Are you available when I need your help?

While I understand that a true open-door policy isn't always possible, it should be easy to find my direct supervisor to ask a question. I need to be able to find you and get my questions answered in a timely manner. We are a team, and I want you to know you can count on me. I need to know I can count on you.

III. Ask My Opinion

Do you ask for my help to solve problems?

As a leader, you may feel like you must always have the answers, but you shouldn't feel that way. No one has all the answers. The truth is, as your employee, I am the one doing the work. I communicate directly with the customers, and I solve their problems every day. I hear what they are saying, both good and bad. There are times you will need my help to answer questions, to solve problems, and to help you design policies and procedures. I want you to know I am happy to help. All you need to do is ask.

IV. Trust Me

Do you have faith in my ability?

I'm a firm believer that you shouldn't need to micromanage people in order to get them to do their job. I can assure you I care about doing a good job, and I always will. I promise to be responsible and to follow company policies and procedures. If I have a question, I will find you and ask for help. I just need you to step back and trust me to do what I am trained to do. I want you to trust me, believe in me, and know you can always count on me.

V. Support Me

Do you care about me as a person?

Illnesses can spring up overnight. Some errands cannot wait until the weekend. Yes, I know my kid was sick last week, but he isn't feeling any better, and we really need to get back to the pediatrician. When an employee works hard for you, please show compassion when inevitable personal issues arise. I assure you, I'm going to feel pretty crummy and nervous about how my personal circumstances are impacting my job and the company. I'll do whatever I can to make it up to the company. I just hope you care enough about me to understand and support me.

|||||||||||||||||||||||||||||||||

The personification of great leadership is the leader who takes more than their share of the blame for failure when things go wrong, while giving their team the majority of the credit for success when things go right.

|||||||||||||||||||||||||||||||||

Ten Key
LEADERSHIP
COMPETENCIES

IIIIIIIIIIIIIIIIIIIIIIIIIIIIII

The true worth of your leadership legacy will be judged, measured, and remembered based upon how well you treated the people around you along the way.

IIIIIIIIIIIIIIIIIIIIIIIIIIIIII

COMPETENCY I: EMPOWERMENT

I just need my supervisor to pay me well, give me work I can enjoy doing, explain the goal to me, and then get out of my way so I can prove I can do it.

—JOHNNY D., GEN Z, PART TIME
RESTAURANT WORKER, OHIO

///////////////////////////////

Empowerment is pushing decision-making downward.

///////////////////////////////

THE IDEA BEHIND EMPOWERING employees is not only giving them the responsibility for performing a task, but going a step further and giving them all the authority and power they need to get the job done—without the need for intervention by a supervisor or manager. I worked for a CEO who was a tremendous leader. He was a big believer in pushing decision-making downward in the organization. He wanted the employees who served the customers to have all the responsibility and authority they needed to make decisions on behalf of customers.

Employee Empowerment

Explain it to me, and I will understand.
     Teach me, and I'll know how.
     Give me a chance, and I'll prove I can do it!

Interestingly, his only real requirements were that employees must always do what is right, do what is fair, and treat customers the way they themselves would reasonably expect to be treated under similar circumstances. His direction to everyone was straightforward and simple. If a customer has a problem, ask: What would you like us to do to resolve this problem? The CEO said, *Then listen to the customer carefully, and whatever the customer says, you are empowered to approve it and implement it if you think their request is fair, right, and reasonable.*

His approach to empowering the employees to serve customers worked flawlessly. The customers were happy with the quality of service, and the employees on the front-line felt they were trusted and respected by the company. The CEO had created a win-win-win scenario for the customers, the employees, and the company.

Do you give employees all the responsibility, authority, and power they need to do their jobs?

That's really what empowerment is all about—delegating decision-making, responsibility, and authority directly to employees. Trusting them to protect company resources while at the same time doing what's right for customers. It's about giving employees the opportunity to make decisions without the need for you as a leader to constantly intervene. When you empower people, you convey confidence in their judgment and abilities.

Ways a leader can empower individuals and teams:

▶ Encourage employees to suggest modifications to the way the work is done to improve productivity.

▶ Get employees to help develop accurate job descriptions to make them more practical and relevant for current and future employees.

▶ Have employees cross-train one another to do the basics of each other's jobs to ensure work continues to flow if an employee is absent.

▶ Encourage employees to sit down with one another to develop efficient solutions to work-flow problems.

▶ Monitor individual and team progress and activities, but avoid interfering unnecessarily.

▶ Have each team create its own structure that dictates how team members process information, schedule work, and efficiently execute duties.

▶ When in doubt, ask the employees what you can do to empower them to more efficiently perform their jobs and serve customers.

The Result: By empowering employees on the front-line, you increase the speed of decision-making as you build each individual's confidence. Efficiency, productivity, and morale can't help but improve. Employees who are empowered feel trusted and respected by the organization's leaders, giving them more pride in everything they do. Empowering employees is a great way to enhance your customer service, and it will help you identify terrific future leaders.

llllllllllllllllllllllllll

An effective leader empowers individuals and team members to make decisions, which builds team synergy.

llllllllllllllllllllllllll

COMPETENCY II: LISTENING

A good leader is sensitive to and listens to the needs of employees, focusing on supporting their needs, wants, and desires, inspiring major results.

—GUILLERMO C., BABY BOOMER, DIRECTOR, MEXICO CITY, MEXICO

|||||||||||||||||||||||||||||||

Listening enhances customer satisfaction, employee productivity, and information sharing between departments, leading to more creative, innovative, and timely solutions.

|||||||||||||||||||||||||||||||

In one of the organizations where I worked, we took listening to employees very seriously. Each year, we surveyed all employees to gather their opinions on how they felt about the quality of the supervision they received from their manager. It's commonly called a 360-degree review.

The anonymous input the employees provided was used in the performance appraisal of their own boss. Now that's serious! All the questions were focused on specific leadership-related questions and scored on a three-tier scale: 1. My manager does not meet my requirements; 2. My manager meets my requirements; and 3. My manager exceeds my requirements. Here are some examples of such employee opinion statements:

- ▶ My manager keeps me informed.
- ▶ My manager communicates clearly.
- ▶ My manager empowers me.
- ▶ My manager teaches me.
- ▶ My manager recognizes my accomplishments.
- ▶ My manager challenges me to perform.
- ▶ My manager is a good listener.
- ▶ My manager supports the team.
- ▶ My manager uses my ideas.
- ▶ My manager responds in a timely manner.
- ▶ My manager encourages cooperation.
- ▶ My manager participates in team activities.
- ▶ My manager sets appropriate priorities.
- ▶ My manager communicates a plan of action.

- ▶ My manager measures my results.
- ▶ My manager believes in fact-finding.
- ▶ My manager is accessible.

Collection of the employee opinion survey scores was only the first step in the process. The second step was a face-to-face group meeting with their manager's boss, who reviewed the results of the survey directly with the employees at a meeting. The manager of the employees was not allowed to be present for this meeting so the employees would feel free to state their honest opinions about their own manager! The employees came away from the experience knowing the company was listening and that their opinions really mattered.

Why is listening, a skill that should come so naturally to humans, so difficult to master?

The art of effective listening simply means knowing and understanding what someone has said to you so that they are convinced you understand their message. Employees know when a leader is listening to them, and they also are perceptive enough to know when their leader is not. Active listening skills are the foundation upon which trust-based relationships are built. Once employees know a leader can be trusted, they know they can count on open, honest, two-way communication.

Ways to listen and respond effectively to employees:

▶ Meet in an area that provides privacy, and stay in the moment by giving the employee your full attention. Close the door and turn off your phone.

▶ When meeting with an employee, start by establishing rapport, which will have a calming effect, then listen to what the employee has to say without interrupting.

▶ Show sincere concern through your facial expressions and body language by nodding, making eye contact, and leaning forward.

▶ Once you have listened to the employee's message, paraphrase what you just heard to show understanding.

▶ When you do talk, use brief verbal affirmations like *I see*, *I know*, *Sure*, or *I understand*.

▶ Get the employee to talk by asking open-ended questions that can't be answered with a yes or no response.

▶ To show understanding, mention similar experiences you've dealt with in the past.

▶ At the end of the meeting, summarize the discussion and the next steps, if any.

The Result: Employees feel their opinions count when they know their supervisor is listening. Effective listening builds mutual respect.

‖‖‖‖‖‖‖‖‖‖‖‖‖‖‖‖‖‖

An effective leader listens to the concerns, ideas, and opinions of employees, which builds a trust-based relationship.

‖‖‖‖‖‖‖‖‖‖‖‖‖‖‖‖‖‖

COMPETENCY III: APPROACHABILITY

A leader is there to guide and serve the team by supporting every individual—not just by giving orders, but by working side by side with them.

—MARTIN L., GEN X, SALES MANAGER,
HAMBURG, GERMANY

ıııııııııııııııııııııııııı

Approachability is the key to building strong relationships with individuals and team members in which trust, confidence, and ideas can flow freely.

ıııııııııııııııııııııııııı

Many of the most-respected corporations in the world have an open-door policy that encourages employees to bring problems, issues, and concerns to their supervisor's attention. Appointments to meet with a company leader are either unnecessary or optional. If the door is open, an employee can walk right in and talk to people! That policy includes the top executives, who are just as accessible, approachable, and welcoming as everyone else. The belief throughout these companies is that openness and accessibility are important to good communication.

Active listening skills are part of the culture, which means people stop what they are doing and give you their full, undivided attention. People in every department support one another because they are all members of the same team.

The goal is for everyone to be approachable in order to enhance internal and external customer service.

Do you make it easy for the people you work with to approach you and communicate with you?

Surprisingly, many leaders create barriers that block effective communications. An approachable leader is a good time manager who is also accessible. He or she makes employees feel comfortable and at ease so they can work together seamlessly without experiencing fear and trepidation. Making yourself accessible to employees gives them a feeling of importance and confidence.

Ways to show you are accessible and approachable:

▶ Stop what you're doing and warmly welcome an employee or anyone else who comes to see you.

▶ Seek out new employees; make certain they know who you are, and make them feel welcome.

▶ Get to know employees before and after meetings by getting to know them as people.

▶ Make a point of talking to people you don't know at company gatherings.

▶ Be accessible outside of group situations for

employees who aren't comfortable speaking to you in front of their peers.

▸ Try to make every interaction with employees positive and even memorable.

▸ Learn and use employees' names to send the message that you value them as individuals.

▸ Listen to employee viewpoints and ideas, even if you don't agree with them, so employees know they can come to you in the future to talk about unpopular or even uncomfortable topics.

The Result: In a company with an employee-centered culture where the supervisors, managers, and executives are easily accessible, employees aren't afraid to approach and talk to or with them about not only their problems and concerns, but also their ideas to improve the company.

ıllıllıllıllıllıllıllıllıllıllıllı

A caring leader is approachable and easily accessible to employees, which helps build strong relationships.

ıllıllıllıllıllıllıllıllıllıllıllı

COMPETENCY IV: MENTORING

The most effective leaders are mentors who respect, teach, train, and positively encourage peers and employees.

—MICHAEL C., GEN Y, ENTREPRENEUR, SHANGHAI, CHINA

‖‖‖‖‖‖‖‖‖‖‖‖‖‖‖‖‖‖‖‖‖‖‖

Mentoring is selflessly sharing your knowledge to help others grow.

‖‖‖‖‖‖‖‖‖‖‖‖‖‖‖‖‖‖‖‖‖‖‖

The definition of *mentor* is someone who acts as a counselor, adviser, teacher, or guide, someone who can be trusted to look out for your best interests. Based on that definition, my parents served as my first mentors. They taught me right from wrong, instilled my work ethic, and gave me the space I needed to grow as an individual. In my career, I can identify, by name, more than thirty different mentors, both women and men, who have positively influenced me by sharing valuable life lessons with me. As you might expect, a few of my mentors are younger than me. Some are my age, and a few are older. I have mentors who influenced me for a short time and moved on, while others have remained constant in my life. My mentors taught me lessons that I still embrace and teach to others today.

Here are several examples of the kinds of lessons I learned from my mentors:

▶ Don't focus on what you can't do; focus on what you can do.

▶ The most important skill is the ability to present your ideas to others.

▶ Don't make excuses or accept excuses from others.

▶ Invest as much energy in your family as you invest in your work.

▶ No matter what you do, strive to be the best.

▶ If you are willing to work hard, you can overcome any adversity.

▶ Find a way to pursue the dream that's planted in your heart.

▶ Believe in others even more than they believe in themselves.

Open your eyes, your ears, and your heart: your potential mentors are all around you, and they're ready to help. You never know who will become your mentors in life, and you can't always predict those for whom you will become a mentor. Every executive, manager, and supervisor has plenty of opportunities to share their knowledge by mentoring future leaders.

IIIIIIIIIIIIIIIIIIIIIIIIIIIIIIIII

Effective leaders are great teachers who willingly share their knowledge, experience, and expertise with others.

IIIIIIIIIIIIIIIIIIIIIIIIIIIIIIIII

Employees need to open themselves up to the transfer of new knowledge and skills in order to create a successful mentor-and-protégé relationship. Learning from an experienced professional is a great way to accelerate your learning.

Do you share your skills, knowledge, and expertise with the people around you to help them unlock their full potential?

Mentoring employees is one of the most important roles of a leader. It is also one of the most personally satisfying. Mentoring creates a symbiotic relationship with employees in which the organization benefits from the improved productivity of employees, while employees benefit by growing and developing their personal skills and knowledge. It is a win-win relationship.

Ways mentoring benefits organizations, leaders, and employees:

- ► Leaders who are mentors selflessly develop the talents of employees.
- ► As employees grow and develop their knowledge, they have a responsibility to act as mentors to other employees.
- ► Mentoring is a way for leaders to leave a legacy, and it's also a way to pay it forward by developing future leaders.
- ► A strong mentor-and-protégé relationship builds the employee's self-confidence.
- ► It helps employees learn to take better control of their work today, while helping clarify career goals.
- ► It encourages employees to speak up and be heard, improving their communication and interpersonal skills.
- ► It teaches employees how to accept and use feedback to improve their job skills and performance.

‖‖‖‖‖‖‖‖‖‖‖‖‖‖‖‖‖‖‖‖‖

For a mentoring-and-protégé relationship to work, it requires not only a willing teacher, but also a willing student.

‖‖‖‖‖‖‖‖‖‖‖‖‖‖‖‖‖‖‖‖‖

The Result: There is no faster way to learn than from an experienced individual who is willing to take you under their wing and teach you what they know. As a leader, you have a responsibility to act as a mentor to employees, to help them learn and grow to become the next generation of leaders.

‖‖‖‖‖‖‖‖‖‖‖‖‖‖‖‖‖‖‖‖‖

A leader's job is to mentor employees to help them grow, which builds an employee's confidence, skills, and know-how.

‖‖‖‖‖‖‖‖‖‖‖‖‖‖‖‖‖‖‖‖‖

COMPETENCY V: EMPATHY

Real leadership is effective, compassionate leadership that leaves employees feeling inspired and refreshed.

—CATHY K., GEN X, MANAGER, HAWAII

||||||||||||||||||||||||||||||

Empathy is showing people you really care about their feelings and concerns.

||||||||||||||||||||||||||||||

Employees struggle with all kinds of personal problems that spill over into the workplace. Those issues generally only become the problem of managers and supervisors when they impact that employee's work or the work of others. Unchecked, one employee's surly attitude, sadness, emotional outbursts, and job performance problems can have a detrimental effect on the morale and productivity of the entire team. For this reason, the manager must figure out what is going on. The first step to resolving employee work-related issues is for the manager to use empathetic listening skills to seek to understand why the employee is feeling and acting in ways that are negatively impacting their work. The second all-important step is for the manager to address the specific performance problem and ask the employee for help to resolve it.

From a leadership standpoint, having empathy doesn't mean adopting an employee's emotional state or accepting excuses. It also doesn't mean coddling or continuing to accept nonperformance. Empathy means the leader thoughtfully considers and understands the feelings of employees during the process of partnering with the employee to resolve the problem. Showing empathy comes easily to leaders who are comfortable sitting down with an employee to openly discuss problems and concerns. The idea behind a leader being empathetic and showing empathy is the concept of *walking in the other person's shoes while continuing to hold employees accountable for performing their jobs at an acceptable level.*

As an HR executive, I had my training department teach our executives, managers, and supervisors to be *empathetic listeners.* We wanted company leaders to listen and respond with empathy to employee concerns. Empathy is the concept of *understanding what the employee is feeling.* To do that, the leader must first identify the employee's emotional state. Only then can the leader show the appropriate concern and response, based on the emotion identified. The employee's emotion could be sadness, anger, fear, aggravation, irritation, resentment, or frustration. Once you understand where the employee is coming from, you as a leader are in a position to show empathy and begin to work with the employee toward resolving the issue, problem, or concern.

We taught our supervisors and managers the delicate balancing act of showing sincere concern for employees experiencing problems while continuing to hold employees accountable for their work. We stressed the importance of not accepting excuses for an employee's unacceptable performance by clearly telling the employee they would be held accountable for doing their job at an acceptable level.

Here is a story illustrating the proper concern a leader should show for an employee experiencing problems while still holding the employee accountable for that unsatisfactory behavior. This story illustrates how a supportive leadership approach often yields a positive outcome:

"I had an employee walk in about forty-five minutes late for work one day. As soon as he came in, he walked up to

me, apologized for his tardiness, and promised to get to work on time in the future. I politely thanked him, but then I told him, "It's the other crew members here you should be apologizing to. It's those employees on the floor that had to work twice as hard to make up for your tardiness; those are the people you should be speaking to." He then walked up to each and every employee and sincerely apologized.

I never want an employee to be afraid of coming to me, as their manager, for fear of being fired; I just want them to know how their actions can have an effect on other workers, so they understand why it is important for them to come to work on time."

—GEOFFREY R., GEN Y, MCDONALDS ASSISTANT MANAGER

When you seek to understand and sincerely empathize with employees' circumstances, you can work together to develop a workable resolution. Often, listening to employees and showing concern is all that is necessary. Employees don't expect you to solve all their problems, and they realize you're not a psychologist who can provide easy answers to their tough questions. Sometimes, the best way a leader can help an employee is just to let the employee talk, listen to them without interrupting, then acknowledge the issue and show you care. The goal from a leader's perspective is building the employee's self-esteem, gaining commitment to resolve any work-related performance problems, and ultimately salvaging an employee who otherwise might fail.

Do you take the time to understand the feelings affecting people on the job?

Compassionate leaders strive to understand and empathize with others. When you show you care by seeking to understand what employees are feeling, you build a relationship based on mutual trust. Once an employee realizes you have considered their thoughts and feelings, they can relax, refocus, and return to work feeling better.

Ways to be an empathetic leader:

▶ Try to understand the employee's point of view when they bring you their issues, problems, concerns, opinions, or ideas.

▶ When the leader and an employee disagree, that leader must seek understanding, not agreement. Both can walk away still disagreeing, but both will clearly understand the *why*.

▶ Ask employees how you can help them, then do whatever you can to pitch in to help achieve a positive outcome.

▶ Displaying an upbeat and positive, supportive attitude when the going gets tough helps reduce the stress level of everybody around you.

▶ Empathetic leadership is showing employees compassion, care, and concern, while still continuing to hold them accountable for performing their jobs at a satisfactory level.

The Result: When you show empathy toward employees, you build respect, trust, and commitment. Showing employees you have concern for their feelings and concerns is one of the best ways a leader can build loyalty and strong relationships. It's not hard to be an empathetic leader; it just takes showing genuine, heartfelt concern for people, being there for employees when they need you, and listening to them when they are facing adversity or tough challenges that impact their life and their job performance.

IIIIIIIIIIIIIIIIIIIIIIIIIII

A compassionate leader is able to empathize with employee concerns, while at the same time holding employees accountable for doing their jobs at an acceptable level, which builds relationships while still reinforcing standards.

IIIIIIIIIIIIIIIIIIIIIIIIII

COMPETENCY VI: INTEGRITY

Concerned and caring leadership means being honest in your dealings, putting the needs of employees before your own, and being there for them when they are facing adversity or tough challenges in their lives or careers.

—MARTHA E., GEN X, GENERAL MANAGER, CALIFORNIA

IIIIIIIIIIIIIIIIIIIIIIIIIIII

Integrity means people can count on you to do what you say you will do when you say you will do it.

IIIIIIIIIIIIIIIIIIIIIIIIIIII

What exactly does it mean when we say someone *has integrity* or *operates with integrity*? Words often used to describe someone who *has integrity* are *honest, trustworthy,* and *reliable.* Your integrity is built when people really know from experience you will always follow through on your commitments. Once your integrity has been established, employees and peers will trust you because they know they can count on you. Your integrity as a leader gives them a feeling of comfort and confidence, especially when you are dealing with them to resolve issues ahead of deadlines.

Integrity is an internally driven choice you make to hold yourself accountable to a set of consistent moral and ethical standards. When a person has integrity, others know they can count on him or her to follow through as promised, with no excuses. Leaders who have integrity also hold others accountable for following through on their commitments.

Early on in my career, I learned a painful lesson about integrity—and lack of integrity—when I failed to live up to one of my commitments. I had a job that required travel. One particular Monday, a day I usually spent in the office, I had an emergency in another city that demanded I go there first thing Monday morning. I left for the airport before dawn and arrived in the late morning at my destination. When I arrived, I checked my email and found a message from my boss asking me where my weekly report was. That report was always due at nine o'clock Monday morning, and I had not sent it. My boss knew about the emergency situation that I was addressing, and he knew that my travel was unplanned. Still, he expected me to deliver on my commitment to turn in my weekly report on time. I had not communicated my intention not to submit my weekly report to him on time!

I responded to his email with one of my own. In it, I reminded him of the crisis situation I was taking care of out of town and gave that as the reason my report was late. I thought I had a bulletproof excuse. My boss responded to my email with a chilling five-word reply, "Where is your weekly report?"

Up to that point in my career, I had always been successful when I came up with reasons or gave excuses for falling short of a goal or a commitment I had made, but not this time. In that moment, I experienced an epiphany, or what is referred to as a *significant emotional event* that has forever changed me. My boss was absolutely right. There are twenty-four hours in a day and 168 hours in a week. I had plenty of time to turn in my report over that prior weekend or on the night before I had to leave on my trip. *I could have hit the deadline for turning in that report and lived up to my commitment, but I had chosen not to.* I figured I would miss the deadline and turn it in later when it was more convenient for me. I was certain my boss would understand.

My boss refused to lower the bar by allowing me to miss that deadline. He was teaching me a valuable lesson about having integrity that I have never forgotten.

From that moment onward, I vowed to live up to my commitments or to proactively communicate to others a valid reason why I would not be able to deliver on a commitment I had made. It was a personal goal to follow through on all my commitments as promised.

Do you ever find yourself making excuses for your own lack of performance? Do you miss deadlines or fail to complete work on time? Do you use hedge phrases like "I'll try," which always leave you room when you fail on a commitment to say, "I told you I'd try"? *As a leader, do you accept excuses from employees when they fail to meet standards?*

When you make excuses for your own lack of performance, you are clearly demonstrating a lack of integrity. Executives, managers, supervisors, and employees who miss deadlines, who fail to live up to commitments, and who make excuses for their failings are unreliable and emotionally dishonest. If you have found yourself making excuses, you can put a stake in the ground starting today, just like I did, by making a commitment to *operate with total integrity* from this day forward.

ıιιιιιιιιιιιιιιιιιιιιιιιιιιιιιιıı

Effective leaders don't make excuses for nonperformance; they can always be counted on to follow through on their commitments!

ıιιιιιιιιιιιιιιιιιιιιιιιιιιιιιıı

It doesn't take long for the people around you to figure out whether you have integrity or not. If you do, you will quickly build strong, trust-based relationships. On the other hand, once employees determine that a leader lacks integrity, there is no way that leader can build a high level of trust with his or her own team. Unfortunately, without integrity, a leader will struggle with relationships and will never be viewed by employees as being a leader they'd willingly choose to follow.

Do you always follow through on the commitments you make to people?

Integrity is a basic requirement or prerequisite for becoming a trusted team leader. Without that trust, nothing else will matter. Not surprisingly, teams more often than not reflect the same values as their leader. If you *operate with integrity*, there's a good chance you have instilled those same values in your team. On the flip side, if you aren't trustworthy and you have proven you don't follow through on your commitments, your team members may not either. Integrity is about creating trust, and trust is the foundation of good leadership.

Ways to demonstrate leadership integrity:

▶ The most common description of integrity is *doing what you say you will do, when you say you will do it.* It's as simple as following through on your commitments every time.

▶ You show integrity when you are honest and open in your dealings with employees, live up to your commitments, and show a willingness to always do what's right.

▶ Leaders are viewed as operating with integrity when they communicate company news, both good and bad, and proactively discuss upcoming organizational changes that impact employees.

▶ When employees are comfortable with company leaders, they are more apt to freely share information.

▶ Leaders have a responsibility to respect the privacy of employees by protecting the confidentiality of information employees have provided to them.

The Result: When you are always honest in your dealings, trustworthy when you make commitments, and prove to the people around you that you can be counted on, you are demonstrating you have integrity. There is no such thing as a lapse in integrity. Lack of integrity is emotional dishonesty at best; at worst, it is outright dishonesty in actions, deeds, and behaviors. Your integrity as a leader is valuable, and it must be guarded judiciously at all times. An honest leader's word is their bond. They always keep their promises, and they deliver results on the commitments they make in a timely manner!

||||||||||||||||||||||||||||

A respected leader has integrity, giving them the right to hold the people around them accountable for following through on their commitments as well.

||||||||||||||||||||||||||||

COMPETENCY VII: ACKNOWLEDGMENT

A leader's job is to remove obstacles impacting the team, support team members when necessary, and recognize employee accomplishments.

—JOSEPH C., GEN X, DISTRICT MANAGER, MASSACHUSETTS

|||||||||||||||||||||||||||||||||

Acknowledgment is sincerely recognizing employees for their contributions to the success of the organization.

|||||||||||||||||||||||||||||||||

The idea behind acknowledging the contributions of employees is the concept of *catching employees who are doing things right.* The beauty of recognizing employees is that it costs nothing in financial terms, yet it pays big dividends in the form of improved morale and productivity. Sincerely delivered appreciation, even just saying thank you, builds the self-esteem of the employee who receives it, as it raises the esprit de corps of the entire team. Plain and simple, when you acknowledge people, you are lifting them up and showing you appreciate their efforts and results. In actuality, it's almost impossible for a leader to give too much recognition; unfortunately, most leaders don't give enough.

In one of my HR jobs, I supported a large corporate accounting function. The employees in accounting focused on accounts payable, accounts receivable, payroll, treasury, tax, data entry, and financial reporting. Due to the size of the company, the employees dealt with a high volume of repetitive, mundane tasks, making the work environment a bit dull and tedious. To create a more enjoyable atmosphere, the accounting leaders worked directly with the employees to develop a variety of nonmonetary methods to reward and recognize individual and team accomplishments.

Each functional area created fun and inspirational contests to make the tedious work required to accomplish goals more enjoyable. In the end, the contests not only achieved the original goal of building the morale of each accounting work group, but also improved the performance of the corporate accounting function as a whole. This is a great example of developing a proactive approach to acknowledging the contributions of employees that also had a positive bottom-line impact!

It's not hard to develop interesting and exciting ways to acknowledge the contributions of employees, and the benefits are significant. Working with your own employees, you can develop a similar customized approach to recognition in your organization.

Human beings have a deep-seated desire to contribute to personally meaningful and worthwhile endeavors, and they want and need those contributions to be recognized. Human nature provides every leader with a great opportunity to build stronger relationships with employees by simply recognizing the success of individuals and teams. As a leader, nothing is more natural than bestowing sincere praise on another individual. The benefits are many, including improved morale, enhanced self-esteem, higher productivity, and teamwork. In addition, your perception as a leader improves when you take the time to acknowledge outstanding contributions of others.

Ways to acknowledge the contributions of employees:

▶ For maximum impact, sincerely recognize the accomplishments of employees in front of their peers.

▶ Let every employee know how important they are to you and to the success of the company by citing specific examples of their contributions.

▶ Reward top-performing employees with challenging new responsibilities as a way of acknowledging their previous success.

▶ Build the self-esteem of employees by complimenting those who demonstrate specific talents, skills, or strengths that you admire.

▶ Thank employees for getting out of their comfort zone by stretching to reach aggressive goals.

▶ Go old school and write a handwritten thank-you note to employees, recognizing them for taking the lead on a project, achieving a difficult goal, or making an exceptional team contribution.

▶ As a sign of your appreciation, provide lunch for team members who are working hard and who otherwise won't get the chance to grab a bite to eat.

▶ If you are running a meeting, keep it short and to the point to show employees you have respect for their valuable time.

▶ When the timing is appropriate, ask employees noninvasive questions about their interests outside work, instead of always focusing interactions with them on business-related topics. This shows you are interested in them as people.

▶ Let your boss know what a great job your team members are doing, and ask your boss to acknowledge your team's accomplishments in writing and face-to-face at meetings.

The Result: When a leader cares enough to acknowledge

an individual or a great team performance by sincerely recognizing accomplishments, the leader gains the respect of every member of their team as they build the self-esteem of each team member.

||||||||||||||||||||||||||||||

A strong leader acknowledges the contributions of employees, which in turn builds loyalty, self-esteem, and pride in their work.

||||||||||||||||||||||||||||||

COMPETENCY VIII: COMMUNICATING

A confident leader has ongoing, open two-way communication with his or her team, resulting in the team members genuinely caring about the leader's vision and the team's success.

—BRIAN M., GEN Y, MANAGER, NEBRASKA

iiiiiiiiiiiiiiiiiiiiiiiiiiiiii

Communication with employees builds respect, trust, understanding, and confidence.

iiiiiiiiiiiiiiiiiiiiiiiiiiiiii

The hallmark of great leaders is their ability to communicate with people one-on-one or in groups. Fortunately, the art of good communication is a skill that can be learned over time, developed and honed by a leader. That is because of all the skills you possess as a leader, none is as important as the ability to present your ideas up, down, and sideways in your organization. In fact, no skill will elevate your stature in your organization more quickly than proving you have the ability to present your ideas articulately to employees and executives alike. The best leaders are thought leaders and outstanding communicators.

From an employee point of view, communication is vital to *feeling in the know*. Sometimes leaders forget how important it is for their team to know and understand what is going on around them. By keeping employees informed, a leader instills confidence in them by alleviating or neutralizing well-founded and unfounded fears. Quality communication breaks down barriers, builds camaraderie, and enhances team commitment. When employees know what's happening around them, they have a better understanding of how they can best help their leader and the company achieve goals. It also eliminates the fear of the unknown, allowing employees to focus their thoughts and attention 100 percent on their jobs.

One of the organizations I worked for had a unique strategy to keep employees informed. Each day, on every work shift, the supervisor of every work group was required to hold a five-minute stand-up meeting with the employees on their team. To understand what I mean by a stand-up meeting, picture a supervisor standing before a group of employees who are standing in a formation not unlike a football huddle. Supervisors in every department were required to hold these stand-up meetings with employees in the office, the manufacturing facility, and the distribution center. In those five-minute, eye-to-eye update meetings, brief two-way information is exchanged to get everyone in the company ready for the workday ahead. Employees are free to ask questions as the supervisor provides job-specific updates and company news. This fast and simple communication technique was a wonderful way to keep employees informed on a daily basis.

Do you take the time to provide regular communication updates so your employees have the information they need to do their jobs?

People in every organization want to feel like they have a good grasp of what's going on in the organization, both inside and outside their work group. As a leader, you have a responsibility to provide timely information to people so they can do their jobs with confidence.

Ways effective leaders communicate:

- ▶ Keep it simple; be clear and concise in your communication to avoid confusion and misunderstanding.
- ▶ There is a strong connection between the quality of your communication and the achievement of your team's performance goals. The better you communicate with your team members, the more likely your team is to achieve its goals.
- ▶ Understand what your employees need to know by asking them if you are giving them all the information they need in a timely fashion.
- ▶ Communicate your messages electronically, in

writing, face-to-face, in conference calls, and at forums and meetings. Your message should be consistent across all these different communication channels.

▶ Prioritize and time your communications so your employees hear good and bad news impacting them from you before they hear about it from others inside or outside the company.

▶ Even with all the technology available today, some information is best delivered via face-to-face communication.

▶ Set up routine, periodic update meetings, and send written communiqués to keep employees informed about how the team is performing and, most importantly, explain what employees can do to help reach targeted objectives.

▶ When you conduct meetings, show you value two-way communication by encouraging employees to ask questions, make comments, or provide their ideas.

The Result: Great leaders find time each day to keep employees informed about activities impacting their work lives. Communication gives employees a feeling of comfort and confidence because they have a good sense of what is going on around them. Keeping them informed also gives employees the feeling that they are important.

IIIIIIIIIIIIIIIIIIIIIIIIIIIIII

A leader's job is to communicate the information employees need to do their jobs, building confidence, which leads to higher levels of achievement.

IIIIIIIIIIIIIIIIIIIIIIIIIIIIII

COMPETENCY IX: HIGH EXPECTATIONS

An effective leader cares passionately about the greatest outcome for others, giving them everything they need so they can achieve great success.

—PERRY J., BABY BOOMER, LOGISTICS
MANAGER, ARKANSAS

High expectations and high standards are the key to goal achievement.

Earlier in my career, one of my mentors taught me one of the great secrets to achieving my lofty personal goals, as well as my team's aggressive goals. What he told me is this: *The secret to achieving goals is to have high expectations and high standards for everything you do.* Through my own experiences over the years, I've learned that he was absolutely right.

Having high expectations and high standards isn't just the key to achieving success in some things, many things, or a lot of things; it is the key to achieving success in everything you do. When I say everything, I quite literally mean everything.

Engaged leaders pursue goals aggressively with focus, discipline, and dogged determination to help their team succeed.

If you are a believer in setting your goals high in life and in business, you won't accomplish them without also having the highest expectations and standards. In fact, most people who fail to reach their full potential in life do so not because they set their goals too high, but because they set their goals too low!

You get what you expect. If you imagine yourself achieving goals that are well within your reach, that don't require you to stretch, in all likelihood, that is exactly what you will accomplish and no more. If, on the other hand, you set your goals so you and your team must stretch to achieve them, you will get there, or you will come pretty darn close. Even if you come up a little short of reaching a lofty goal, you are miles ahead of where you would have been if you and your team had set easily attainable targets.

Do you always maintain the highest standards for yourself and your team?

Great leaders dream big dreams and set lofty goals. They have high expectations for themselves and for everyone else on their team. In setting team goals, the team leader should work directly with team members, and together they set what are called "stretch goals." A *stretch goal* cannot be achieved by small performance improvements; it requires you to *stretch* and reach in order to achieve the goal.

IIIIIIIIIIIIIIIIIIIIIIIIIIIIII

When experienced leaders set goals, they set big goals, because they know the tendency for many people is to set their goals far too low!

IIIIIIIIIIIIIIIIIIIIIIIIIIIIII

Goal attainment requires every team member to have high standards, a strong work ethic, and total commitment. The key to achieving aggressive goals starts with a well-communicated plan of action, followed by superior tactical execution. Ninety percent of what it takes to achieve any strategy is the execution of it. Having a combination of high expectations, high standards, and disciplined execution are the keys to achieving at the highest levels.

Ways a leader can demonstrate high expectations and high standards:

▶ A great way to set goals is by getting individual team members to help set their own goals. Most employees will actually set their goals higher than you would have set them.

▶ Believe in the capabilities of everyone on the team, and then set the performance bar high. Most people have withheld potential that a great leader can draw out.

▶ Focus the team on continuous improvement, continuous learning, striving for excellence, and quality in everything they do.

▶ To achieve lofty goals, sometimes you and your team need to get out of your comfort zone and challenge your approach to your existing strategy. When you do, you may discover an even better and more efficient way to achieve your goals.

▶ Set goals that are difficult to reach, and you may be surprised by how much more your team can accomplish.

The Result: The good news for every leader is that the decision to prosper at the highest level is a matter of personal choice. You can make the decision today to become the very best at what you do, and you can challenge your team to do the same. If you maintain high standards coupled with high expectations for success, you will create your own self-fulfilling prophecy for your personal success and your team's success as well!

ıılıılıılıılıılıılıılıılıılıı

A confident leader has high expectations and high standards for their team and themselves, which ultimately leads to outstanding performance.

ıılıılıılıılıılıılıılıılıılıı

COMPETENCY X: LEADING BY EXAMPLE

Acting as a teacher, nurturer, and contributor, a real leader raises people up by stepping down from a position of authority to work directly with team members.

—KIRBY E., BABY BOOMER, SUPERVISOR, MINNESOTA

ıılıılıılıılıılıılıılıılıılıı

Lead by example, and your actions will always speak louder than your words.

ıılıılıılıılıılıılıılıılıılıı

When a leader *leads by his or her own example*, they literally model the same behaviors that they expect to see from their team members. Simply put, the leader sets a good example that the employees are expected to follow. That sounds good in theory, but many leaders find it difficult to live up to it in practice. The challenge, especially for leaders, is the idea of saying one thing to employees while the company's executives, managers, and supervisors do another.

A classic example of a double standard is executives issuing an expense-control "pinch pennies" directive that requires cost reductions across the board, impacting employees and work groups, while executives continue to fly first class, stay at five-star hotels, buy lavish meals, and ride around town in limousines.

If a leader assumes employees won't notice the double standard, that leader needs to think again. Any time a company's leaders ask employees to follow a strict policy or adhere to a high standard while the leaders follow a less stringent or different standard, the employees always find out. The result is a negative reaction and lower morale, leading to productivity problems and even employee turnover.

That's the whole point of *leading by example*. What you say to employees and what you do as a leader need to mirror each other. An honest leader would never take advantage of their position and hold themselves to a different or lower standard than what they expect of their team members.

Interestingly, by observing their leader's ABCs—such as practicing self-restraint, operating with integrity and discipline, and practicing caring and respect for others—the employees begin to emulate, develop, and model those same traits and characteristics. In the process, the entire team begins to work toward the good of the whole because this approach is in the best interest of all. Leading by example, the leader ends up influencing everyone on the team to embrace the same values.

Do you model the behaviors you hope and expect everyone else will follow?

As a leader, you have a responsibility to set a good example for your team. Employees look to you for guidance and strength, and they are watching to see if what you say matches what you do. By setting the example, you show your team, through your actions and behaviors, exactly what is expected of them. When you lead by example, you make it easy for others to follow you.

Ways to show you lead by your own example:

- ▶ When the manager is holding the team to the same standards followed by all company leaders, the employees will follow their example.

- ▶ A good leader actually holds himself or herself accountable to a higher standard than what is expected of the employees on their team.

- ▶ Leaders are busy people and so are employees; it is important to make time to work alongside your team. It is through your actions that you prove you are committed to the team's success.

- ▶ When the team or a team member makes a mistake, it doesn't matter who made the mistake. A great leader takes responsibility, fixes the problem, and moves on.

- ▶ Put the needs of your team ahead of your own, show them the way, and they will willingly choose to follow you.

- ▶ Your actions speak louder than your words; don't ever forget your team is watching your every move, so you always need to follow the same rules you set for them.

The Result: When you lead by example, you follow the same rules expected of your team. As a result, you build trust, and your team respects you as a leader.

|||||||||||||||||||||||||||||||||

Outstanding leaders lead by example by holding themselves to the same or even higher standards than those expected of others, which builds the feelings of equality and fairness.

|||||||||||||||||||||||||||||||||

RICHARD BRANSON, A WIDELY respected leadership guru, serial entrepreneur, and CEO of the Virgin Group, believes his sixty-five thousand employees are the company's top priority.[19] He is surprised more companies haven't adopted an employee-centered culture strategy. Branson says his priorities at Virgin Group are employees first, customers second, and shareholders third. When asked why he believes putting employees first is so important to his business, Branson responded, "Customer service can make or break a business. If you treat your staff well, they will be happy. Happy staff are proud staff, and proud staff deliver excellent customer service, which drives business success."[20] The point Richard Branson makes is quite simple; leaders need to put their employees first so the employees feel comfortable putting the customers first.

Putting employees first and creating an employee-centered culture could not succeed at the Virgin Group or at any other company without top-to-bottom leadership commitment. It takes the CEO, president, executives, managers, and supervisors all making a commitment to changing the way people are led. In order for an *employee-first cultural initiative* to take hold, the top executives, including the CEO, must take the lead by modeling the appropriate leadership behaviors expected from everyone else. *Why is that important?* Showing sincere concern for and supporting the needs of employees is a self-actualized behavior.

In order for leaders to demonstrate those behaviors, they must have high self-esteem. Supervisors on the front line cannot project positive values and correct behaviors to employees without feeling good about how their bosses are treating them. That is the reason managers and supervisors must be treated by the leaders above them in the same supportive manner as they are expected to treat the employees reporting to them.

Executives can't say one thing while doing another and expect to improve employee engagement. Until the organization's top executives and the CEO or president buy into *putting the needs of employees first*, a systemic *employee-centered cultural initiative* isn't sustainable.

Enhancing Customer Service, Revenue Growth, and Profitability

The emotional connection an employee feels toward their employer, supervisor, and job ultimately determines his or her short- and long-term commitment level toward that supervisor, that job, and that company's goals.

When an employees-first cultural initiative is actually rolled out in a company, the ABCs of leaders grow and expand rapidly—like wildfire—into every corner of the organization. The company's culture experiences a truly amazing and powerful transformation that, once started, is virtually impossible to stop. All the withheld potential of people, employees, and leaders comes pouring out, and the company reaps the benefits in the form of higher morale and productivity, enhanced customer service, top-line revenue growth, and bottom-line profitability. Once this initiative is established, there is no turning back, because employee-focused leadership values quickly become buried deep inside the DNA of the company's culture and its leaders. As the initiative gains traction, previous problems associated with the lack of employee engagement will quickly disappear.

Employee Engagement and Retention Model

This chart illustrates the steps required for effective leaders to retain an engaged workforce, one employee at a time.

EMPLOYEES FIRST ACTION PLAN

The final and most important question is *how can a company get a "putting your employees first" cultural initiative started?* There are a number of key steps and specific activities that a leadership team must focus on to fully engage employees and positively impact employee retention. Here are just some of them.

▶ **Commit to Employee Engagement**: Company leaders first need to understand the employee engagement and retention steps described previously, as well as their leadership role in creating an employee-focused culture. These steps provide an excellent illustration of the role every leader plays in the creation of a high-performing, people-first culture.

▶ **Identify Your Cultural Values**: Make sure leaders embrace a core set of organizational values toward people that include supporting others, empowering employees, respecting people, valuing relationships, inspiring trust, communicating values, and engaging employees. Employees will sense through each leader's actions whether they genuinely embrace

those values. Employees will hold leaders accountable for living up to the corporate people values.

▶ **Train Company Leaders**: Prior to the official rollout
to employees, company leaders are trained on a
specific set of cultural values, along with a description of expected leadership Actions, Beliefs, and
Competencies. Teach the leadership team the importance of developing strong interpersonal relationships with every team member. Leaders are asked
to get to know people beyond what they contribute
to the company through their work. As a start, learn
their interests, goals, and aspirations. Taking the time
to get to know every employee pays big dividends.
When the company or the work group faces adversity, major challenges, or catastrophic problems,
the ability to leverage those relationships can be the
difference between great success and abysmal failure.

▶ **Announce the Change**: Once the leadership team
has been trained, the CEO makes an organizational
announcement discussing the company's commitment to engaging employees and implementing an
employee-centered culture. It is a top-down change
strategy. Keep in mind that organizational change is

difficult because you are attempting to change the attitudes, behaviors, and engrained experiences of so many leaders. Expect some level of cynicism and resistance to change from leaders at all levels. When it happens, deal with it one-on-one.

▸ **Conduct Meetings with Employees**: Have top leaders hold meetings with all employees to explain the company's commitment to the new employee-first cultural initiative.

▸ **Survey Employee Opinions**: On a periodic basis, company leaders should proactively survey employee opinions and perceptions of their current leadership, their work environment, and their jobs. In the process, company leaders will learn not only what is important to employees, but also the employee satisfaction level with the company and its leaders. When problems are identified via the survey process, solutions should be developed, with the involvement of both the employees and that work group's leader. Follow-up must be done to ensure improvements or resolutions to the problems identified have actually been completed. Employee opinion surveys are an excellent method for providing leaders with

360-degree feedback to help them develop their leadership skills. I've always found that employees provide thoughtful, fair feedback when their opinions are surveyed.

▶ **Increase Communication**: Develop an ongoing employee-focused communication campaign so employees always feel connected to what is happening in the organization. In addition, when workgroup changes are being considered, leaders need to review them before implementation with the employees affected, carefully taking into account employee input.

▶ **Reward and Recognize**: Create a monetary and/or nonmonetary reward-and-recognition program so leaders systemically *catch employees doing things right*. Have company leaders hold periodic scheduled and unscheduled meetings to acknowledge the contributions of individuals and teams. Send thank-you notes to employee's homes so family members understand how much employees are appreciated.

▶ **Seek Understanding**: Implement rules, policies, and procedures—with employee input prior to implementation—so employee ideas can be incorporated into the final product. Though employees may not fully agree, in the end, they will understand why. That emphasis on getting employees to understand popular and unpopular decisions creates a perception of fairness.

▶ **Encourage Two-Way Communication**: Implement an open-door policy so employees feel free and safe walking into their supervisor's office to voice their opinions on any subject they feel strongly about. Proactively encourage employees to communicate with all levels of the organization. Make it okay for employees to agree to disagree with company policies, procedures, and practices. The goal for leaders should always be to seek understanding, not agreement.

▶ **Gather Employee Ideas**: Tap into the intellectual horsepower of employees by asking them for their opinions, ideas, and solutions to solve organizational problems impacting their work. It's no surprise the people closest to the actual work always have the best solutions. The funny thing is, if leaders don't ask them for their input, the employees may or may not volunteer their ideas or solutions.

▶ **Evaluate Current Staffing**: Well-intentioned people are sometimes placed in the wrong job, one that fails to leverage their particular talents. In most organizations, when that happens, the employee ends up quitting or being fired for poor performance. The simple solution is to identify those misfits and move them into roles that leverage their strengths. It's a win-win for the company and the employee; it's also good for team morale.

▶ **Focus on Individual and Team Development**: In an employee-centered culture, a leader's primary job is focusing on the needs of employees by helping them reach their full potential and by assisting them to achieve company goals. The best executives, managers, and supervisors have a knack for bringing out the hidden potential in people and for selflessly developing promotable talent for the company. Leaders who are skilled at training and developing people are the kind employees really want to work with. They're also the kind of leaders who tend to get noticed and promoted. By investing in developing the skills, abilities, and knowledge of your own employees, you build loyalty and commitment.

So what can you do as an individual if your organization's top leaders aren't willing to change and adopt the values necessary for the creation of a systemic employee-centered culture? You can choose to be the change in your organization that you want to see. You can make the choice to become a strong leader of people in your sphere of influence, focusing on the employees closest to you. By putting the members of your team first, you can prove to the other leaders around you—by your actions and results—that focusing on the needs of employees has a positive effect on your team's morale and performance.

If your organization is willing to make a commitment to people by putting employees first, your company will create a sustainable competitive advantage in the marketplace. More importantly, your company's leaders will be on the right path to becoming highly effective leaders!

ACKNOWLEDGMENTS

I want to thank each of the following managers and employees from around the world who provided the leadership quotes and employee perspectives included in this book.

Brian M.—Manager, Nebraska

Cathy K.—Manager, Hawaii

Geoffrey R.—Assistant Manager, Florida

Guillermo C.—Director, Mexico City, Mexico

Johnny D.—Restaurant Worker, Ohio

Joseph C.—District Manager, Massachusetts

Kirby E.—Supervisor, Minnesota

Maranda G.—Office Staff, Illinois

Martha E.—General Manager, California

Martin L.—Sales Manager, Hamburg, Germany

Michael C.—Entrepreneur, Shanghai, China

Perry J.—Logistics Manager, Arkansas

ENDNOTES

1   Paul Kiewiet, "What Does It Take to Engage Employees?" *Promo Marketing*, April 28, 2011, http://magazine.promomarketing .com/post/what-does-it-take-engage-employees/all/.

2   Mitra Toossi, "Labor force projections to 2024: the labor force is growing, but slowly," *Monthly Labor Review*, U.S. Bureau of Labor Statistics, December 2015, https://doi.org/10.21916/mlr.2015.48.

3   "Workplace Redefined: Shifting Generational Attitudes During Economic Change," *Robert Half International*, 2014, 10. https://www.roberthalf.com/sites/default/files/Media_Root /RobertHalf_WorkplaceRedefined.pdf.

4   Mitra Toossi, "Labor force projections to 2020: a more slowly growing workforce," *Monthly Labor Review*, U.S. Bureau of Labor Statistics (January 2012): 43–64, https://www.bls.gov/opub /mlr/2012/01/art3full.pdf.

5   Diana Farrel, Eric Beinhocker, Ezra Greenberg, Suruchi Shukla, Jonathan Ablett, Geoffrey Greene, "Talkin' 'Bout My

Generation: The Economic Impact of Aging US Baby Boomers," McKinsey Global Institute (June 2008): 38, http://www .mckinsey.com/global-themes/employment-and-growth/talkin -bout-my-generation.

6   Leah McGrath Goodman, "Millennial College Graduates: Young, Educated, Jobless," *Newsweek*, May 27, 2015, http://www .newsweek.com/2015/06/05/millennial-college-graduates-young -educated-jobless-335821.html.

7   Sarah Sladek, *Knowing Y: Engaging the Next Generation Now* (Association Management Press, 2014), 6.

8   Carol Phillips, "Gen Y: Our Values Define Us," *Millennial Marketing*, February 9, 2010, http://www.millennialmarketing .com/2010/02/gen-y-our-values-define-us/.

9   Jeanne C. Meister and Karie Willyerd, *The 2020 Workplace* (Harper Business, 2010), quoted in JVanBroekhoven, "The Generational Workforce of the Future," *Hogan Assessments*, June 18, 2012, http://www.hoganassessments.com/the-gener ational-workforce-of-the-future/.

10   "State of the American Workplace," Gallup Inc. (February 2017): 61, http://news.gallup.com/reports/199961/state-american-work place-report-2017.aspx.

11   "Employee Job Satisfaction and Engagement: Revitalizing a Changing Workforce," *The Society for Human Resource Management*,

2016, 57. https://www.shrm.org/hr-today/trends-and-forecasting /research-and-surveys/Documents/2016-Employee-Job-Satisfaction -and-Engagement-Report.pdf.

12 Terry R. Bacon, "What People Want from Relationships: A Research Study," Lore International Institute (November 2006): 7.

13 Bacon, "What People Want from Relationships: A Research Study," 7.

14 "The 2014 Global Workforce Study: Driving Engagement Through a Consumer-Like Experience," Towers Watson (August 2004): 5, https://www.towerswatson.com/en/Insights/IC-Types/Survey -Research-Results/2014/08/the-2014-global-workforce-study.

15 Andrew J. Oswald, Eugenio Proto, and Daniel Sgroi, "Happiness and Productivity," *Journal of Labor Economics* 33, no. 4 (October 2015): 789–822, https://doi.org/10.1086/681096.

16 Jamie Doward, "Happy people really do work harder," *Guardian* (US edition), July 10, 2010, https://www.theguardian.com /science/2010/jul/11/happy-workers-are-more-productive.

17 Oswald, "Happiness and Productivity," 789–822.

18 Gallup Inc, "State of the American Workplace," 61.

19 Richard Branson, "Learn to look after your staff first and the rest will follow," Virgin Group, October 29, 2014, https://www.virgin .com/richard-branson/staff-come-first.

20 Branson, "Learn to look after your staff first and the rest will follow."

BIBLIOGRAPHY

Bacon, Terry R. "What People Want from Relationships: A Research Study." Lore International Institute (November 2006).

Branson, Richard. "Learn to look after your staff first and the rest will follow." Virgin Group, 29 October 2014. https://www.virgin.com/richard-branson/staff-come-first.

Doward, Jamie. "Happy people really do work harder." *Guardian* (US Edition), 10 July 2010. https://www.theguardian.com/science/2010/jul/11/happy-workers-are-more-productive.

Farrel, Diana, Eric Beinhocker, Ezra Greenberg, Suruchi Shukla, Jonathan Ablett, and Geoffrey Greene. "Talkin' 'Bout My Generation: The Economic Impact of Aging US Baby Boomers." McKinsey Global Institute (June 2008): 38. http://www.mckinsey.com/global-themes/employment-and-growth/talkin-bout-my-generation.

Gallup Inc. "State of the American Workplace." February 2017.

http://news.gallup.com/reports/199961/state-american
-workplace-report-2017.aspx.

Goodman, Leah McGrath. "Millennial College Graduates: Young, Educated, Jobless." *Newsweek*, 27 May 2015. http://www .newsweek.com/2015/06/05/millennial-college-graduates -young-educated-jobless-335821.html.

Kiewiet, Paul. "What Does It Take to Engage Employees?" *Promo Marketing*, 28 April 2011. http://magazine .promomarketing.com/post/what-does-it-take-engage -employees/all/.

Meister, Jeanne C. and Karie Willyerd. *The 2020 Workplace*. New York: Harper Business, 2010. Quoted in J VanBroekhoven. "The Generational Workforce of the Future." *Hogan Assessments*, 18 June 2012. http://www.hoganassessments .com/the-generational-workforce-of-the-future/.

Oswald, Andrew J., Eugenio Proto, and Daniel Sgroi. "Happiness and Productivity." *Journal of Labor Economics* 33, no. 4 (2015): 789–822. https://doi.org/10.1086/681096.

Phillips, Carol. "Gen Y: Our Values Define Us." *Millennial Marketing*, 9 February 2010. http://www.millennialmarketing .com/2010/02/gen-y-our-values-define-us/.

Robert Half International. "Workplace Redefined: Shifting Gen erational Attitudes During Economic Change." 2014, 10.

https://www.roberthalf.com/sites/default/files/Media_Root/RobertHalf_WorkplaceRedefined.pdf.

Sladek, Sarah. *Knowing Y: Engaging the Next Generation Now*. Washington, DC: Association Management Press, 2014.

The Society for Human Resource Management. "Employee Job Satisfaction and Engagement: Revitalizing a Changing Workforce." 2016, 57. https://www.shrm.org/hr-today/trends-and-forecasting/research-and-surveys/Documents/2016-Employee-Job-Satisfaction-and-Engagement-Report.pdf.

Toosi, Mitra. "Labor force projections to 2020: a more slowly growing workforce." *Monthly Labor Review*, U.S. Bureau of Labor Statistics, January 2012. https://www.bls.gov/opub/mlr/2012/01/art3full.pdf.

———"Labor force projections to 2024: the labor force is growing, but slowly." *Monthly Labor Review*, U.S. Bureau of Labor Statistics, December 2015. https://doi.org/10.21916/mlr.2015.48.

Towers Watson. "The 2014 Global Workforce Study: Driving Engagement Through a Consumer-Like Experience." August 2004. https://www.towerswatson.com/en/Insights/IC-Types/Survey-Research-Results/2014/08/the-2014-global-workforce-study.

ABOUT THE AUTHOR

Michael Bergdahl, SPHR is a professional international business speaker, author, and turnaround specialist. He worked for twenty-five years in human resources for *Fortune* 1000 companies including Walmart, where he was director of people for the headquarters office and worked directly with Walmart founder Sam Walton; PepsiCo, Group HR Manager; Waste Management, VPHR; and American Eagle Outfitters, VPHR. He also worked as a Plant HR & Safety Manager at J. M. Huber, a privately owned $2 billion manufacturing company, and received Senior Professional in Human Resources (SPHR) lifetime certification from SHRM.

He started his career in his family's Houston, Texas-based publishing business as HR Director. As a turnaround specialist, he has participated in two successful business turnarounds at public companies. In addition, he has written five books, including *What I Learned from Sam Walton: How to Compete and Thrive in a Walmart World* (John Wiley, 2004, published in ten languages). He is a graduate of the Pennsylvania State University with a bachelor of arts degree in sociology and behavioral science.

Michael Bergdahl is a husband, father, caregiver, servant leader, HR guru, writer, speaker, and mentor. Michael and his family live on a farm in Pennsylvania. To book Michael to present *Putting Your Employees First* as a keynote speaker or workshop leader for your next conference or meeting, contact Michael Bergdahl Associates, LLC, at michaelbergdahl.net.

LEARN WHAT TYPE OF LEADER YOU TRULY ARE!

We have created a FREE self-assessment to gauge how committed you are to becoming a more effective leader of people by putting employees first. This self-assessment will give you a snapshot of the effectiveness of your current style of leadership. With the purchase of this title, you can access this FREE fantastic resource and more through Simple Truths!

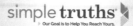